Teacher Edition
Writer's Companion
Support and Practice for Writing
Grade 1

Contents

The Traits of Good Writing

To play a game well, children need to use special skills and strategies. In baseball, for example, a player needs to hit well, catch well, and run quickly. Good writing takes special skills and strategies, too. This web shows the traits, or characteristics, of good writing, which are the foundation for the lessons in this book.

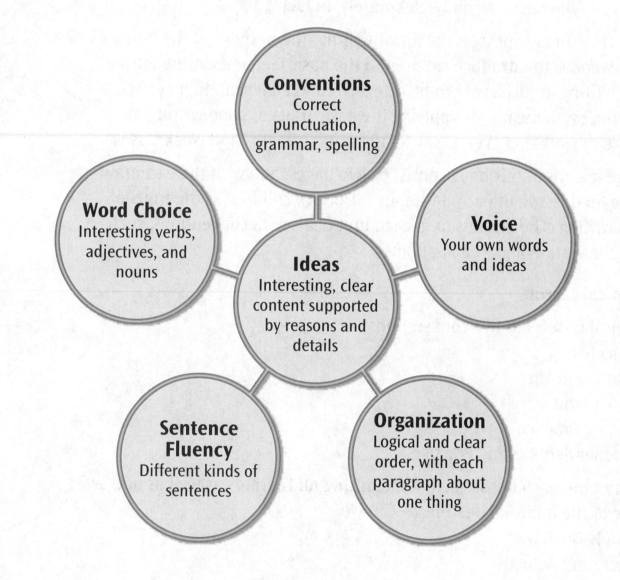

Introduction

Children at the primary level are eager to communicate, and they love to write, even though most of their writing is frequently without conventions that enable us to read it easily. From the time they begin to scribble on paper, children are "writing" with a purpose. If you ask them what a piece of their work is about, they usually will be more than happy to tell you, often quite elaborately, in fact.

Since they already possess the joy of writing, the purpose of the *Writer's Companion* is to introduce children to the basic elements. Although most writing at this level can be categorized as *emergent,* there exists, nonetheless, a means for applying the basic traits of good writing to children's work and even a way to assess its strengths and weaknesses.

All the lessons in this book consist of two pages, and with the exception of the final lesson of each unit, they introduce children to the traits of good writing. The last lesson in each unit deals with conventions, such as capitalization and punctuation.

A Typical Lesson

A typical lesson has five core sections:
- Objectives
- Oral Warm-Up
- Teach/Model
- Guided Practice
- Independent Writing Practice

In addition, each lesson includes Reaching All Learners as well as one or more of the following features:
- Hands-On Activity
- Literature Activity
- Sharing and Discussing
- Extra Practice

Emergent Writing

Most children enter Grades K and 1 as emerging writers. They realize that words can be written and read by themselves or others. Even though all children want to be able to write, they will enter school at different levels. Knowing what to look for and interpreting what you see will help you follow children's learning and make appropriate instructional decisions.

Beginning writers progress through predictable, recognizable stages of spelling development that vary in duration for individual children. Since these stages are not rigid, examples from more than one of the following stages will often appear in the same piece of writing.

Stages of Writing/Spelling

- **Scribbling,** or pretend writing, is probably a child's first attempt at print. A child at this stage can often tell you exactly what his or her symbols mean.

- **Letter Strings,** or random letters, are a child's first attempt at using the letters of the alphabet. At this stage, letters do not yet represent sounds. The child often uses capital letters and may also be practicing left-to-right and top-to-bottom progression on the page.

- **One-letter spelling** is a common occurrence in early writing. The child is more aware of the letter sounds. He or she will often use the initial consonant, and maybe another distinctive consonant, to represent the entire word, such as *c* for *cat.*

- **Phonetic spelling** is the stage where the child shows an understanding of sound-symbol correspondences. The child should be encouraged to sound out words. He or she can often determine the initial, final, and sometimes medial consonant sounds of a word. Vowel sounds usually come much later.

- **Transitional spelling** is the stage in which children adjust their own spelling rules to accommodate what they are learning from their reading. Children at this stage will start to use features such as double consonants and silent letters.

- **Conventional spelling** begins to appear with the use of a few high-frequency words. As the child continues writing, more and more words are written with conventional spelling.

LESSON 1
Choosing a Topic

OBJECTIVES
- To use pictures and objects to stimulate imagination
- To use questions to generate ideas for writing
- To find a topic of interest

Oral Warm-Up   Display a shoe. Then say:

> **Make believe I just found this shoe. Looking at the shoe gives me all kinds of ideas. What if my friend lost this shoe? What if a *toy bear* lost this shoe? How do you think that might have happened? What do you think might happen because of that?**

Ask volunteers how a friend might have lost a shoe. Ask other volunteers how a toy bear might have lost the shoe. Encourage children to let their imaginations run free, imagining various possibilities for each situation. Then ask other volunteers to suggest different questions that come to their minds about the shoe.

Teach/Model   Tell children that writers look at things in interesting ways, and they are always asking themselves questions about the things they see and hear. Explain that these questions often give writers ideas—or topics—to write about.

Direct children's attention to pages 18–19 of *The Hat*. Model the process of asking questions to generate a writing topic, pausing as you ask each question to allow children time to make suggestions.

> **Model**   **I have many ideas and questions as I look at these pictures. For example: What if Dan doesn't catch the hat? What if the dog catches it? What if the wind blows the hat far away? Where will it go? Who will find it? How will Dan feel? How will Pam feel?**

Encourage children to use their imaginations as they think about the hat. Then ask them what questions come to their minds as they look at the pictures. Listen carefully to each suggestion, encouraging children to make up brief "stories" as they try to answer their own questions. Explain that asking questions in this way helps your imagination run free. Point out that thinking about how to answer those questions is exactly how many writers get ideas for what to write about.

HANDS ON ACTIVITY: WHERE, OH WHERE?

Materials: shoebox and pictures of different locations, such as beaches, lakes, and mountains

Directions:

1. Place pictures face down in a shoebox. Have children sit in a circle.
2. Pull a picture from the box. Show the picture. Then name the location and ask a question about what might happen there. For example, say: *This is a lake. What if a girl saw a huge boat in the lake?*
3. Invite a volunteer to think of another *What if . . .* question about the picture. After giving that child time to ask and answer his or her question, invite another child to respond to the picture.
4. Continue with other pictures, allowing two or three volunteers to pose the questions that come to their minds for each one.
5. Summarize the activity by explaining that looking at pictures and objects and asking questions about them is a good way for a writer to get ideas to write about.

Guided Practice Remind children of all the questions that had come up about the picture of the hat. Challenge children to recall and describe some of them. Then explain that a good way to use these ideas would be to draw pictures of them. Say:

> **Let's see. What if the dog catches the hat? What would happen? Would he eat the hat? Probably not. But he might run around with it in his mouth. And I bet Dan would try to catch the dog in order to get the hat back. That could look very silly, couldn't it? Let's see if I can draw that.**

Draw a picture on the board illustrating the scene you have just described. Point out and explain each element as you draw it. Then have children choose a question and a scene of their own and draw it. Encourage and compliment children as they work. Provide help as needed, such as possible questions and ways to draw their scenes.

Independent Writing Practice **Ask a Question:** Display the shoe from the beginning of the lesson as well as several other common objects, such as an eraser, a coat, a toy, a book, and so on. Remind children of all the wonderful ideas they had about the shoe. Then have each child choose an object and think of a question about it that could make for an interesting story or other piece of writing. Have children work on their own to make a drawing of that question and encourage them to write whatever words they can about their object and question.

★ Extra Practice

Have pairs use common classroom items to role-play skits. Tell one child to hold up an item and ask, *What if . . .* Have the other child use words and actions to role-play a response. Then have children choose another item and switch roles.

Reaching All Learners

BELOW LEVEL	ADVANCED	ENGLISH LANGUAGE LEARNERS
Before children begin the Independent Writing Practice, use additional pictures or objects to help them develop their ability to generate ideas. If necessary, prompt them with *What if . . .* questions as starters.	Have children think of additional questions as they generate ideas during the Independent Writing Practice. Tell them to ask questions that begin with *when, where, who,* and *how.* Have them provide additional drawings and words to express the questions.	Make certain English language learners understand the meaning of *What if . . .* Clarify the meaning of the phrase by explaining that a *What if . . .* question is not about something that has really happened. Instead, it is about something a person imagines could happen.

© Harcourt

LESSON 2
Narrowing a Topic

OBJECTIVES
- To understand how to narrow topic ideas
- To narrow topic ideas
- To write topics

Oral Warm-Up   Tell children that they will play an idea game. Then say:

Let's play "I'm Thinking About a Sport." The sport is baseball. You play this sport with a bat and a ball and a glove. Who else is thinking about a sport? What sport is it? How do you play it? What do you need in order to play it?

Invite children to name a sport and tell something about it. Write a list of the sports on chart paper. Have children give details about their chosen sports, using the form, "My sport is _____. To play it, you _____. You need _____." Praise children as they make their suggestions and encourage as many children as possible to participate.

Teach/Model   Ask children if they would like to write about sports. Then say:

I would like to write about sports. But there is so much to write about! Think of all the sports we just talked about—and all the rules and equipment. How could we write about all of that?

Explain that writers take a big idea like *sports* and make it smaller and smaller until it becomes just the right size for a topic. Display a flour sifter and talk with children about how you pour something into the top of the sifter, turn it, and smaller pieces come out the other end. Explain that we can use a sifter to make ideas small enough to write about.

Model   The sifter will help us take a big idea and make it small enough to write about. Here goes my big idea—*sports*—into the sifter. I turn the crank and smaller ideas come out. Let's see now. We put in our big idea—*sports*, and out comes a smaller idea—*what happened when I went swimming at a pool last summer.* Now I have a topic to write about!

Have children suggest smaller ideas related to sports. Discuss their suggestions, talking about why the smaller ideas would be good topics for their writing. Summarize by reminding children that it is very difficult to write about a really big idea, so writers have to find a smaller part of an idea to write about.

HANDS ON ACTIVITY: MAKE IT SMALLER

Materials: flour sifter, magazine picture, manila paper, and scissors

Directions:

1. Provide a detailed magazine picture glued to manila paper. Ask children to describe the big ideas they have as they look at the big picture. Turn the sifter several times, explaining that you are making the big picture smaller. Cut the picture into smaller recognizable pieces, such as characters or objects.

2. Have a child choose one of the small pictures and discuss how it makes the big idea from the big picture smaller. Tell children they can do the same thing by thinking about ways to make their topic ideas smaller.

3. Continue with additional pieces of the picture.

Guided Practice   Direct children's attention to pages 32–33 of *Sam and the Bag*. Ask children what big ideas come to mind as they look at the pictures. Write each idea on a piece of paper. Then invite children to say, *Sift It!* Ask children what smaller ideas might come out of the funnel. If necessary, prompt children by pointing out that, for example, the big ideas *Animals* or *Parties* might come from the pictures. Ask:

> **What smaller idea do you think I could get if I put the idea *Animals* through the sifter? What if I put *Parties* into it?**

Help children recognize that topics such as *Dogs That Rescue People, My Pet Parakeet,* or *My Birthday Party Last Year* all would be topics that could come out of the sifter. Write children's suggested topics on the board and read them to the class. Encourage children to discuss what they would write about for each topic. Then say:

> **Now I'll make a poster telling everyone what my topic is.**

Choose a topic for yourself and share it with the class. Then make a drawing (or paste cut-out magazine pictures) related to your topic on a piece of colored paper. On the paper write the title of the topic, saying each word aloud as you write it. Then display your poster, and tell children that they'll get a chance later on to make their own posters.

Independent Writing Practice   **Narrowing Topics:** Have children take turns using the sifter to come up with ideas and narrow them into writing topics. Remind them that they might start out with a big idea like *Holidays* and sift it until they have a narrower topic such as *What We Did at Our July 4th Picnic*. Distribute colored paper and have each child create a poster telling what his or her topic is. Encourage children to include a picture of some kind on their posters as well as any words that might help people identify the topic.

> **SHARING AND DISCUSSING**
>
> Give children a big idea, such as *School, Hobbies,* or *Friends,* and have them act out pouring the big idea into the sifter, and finding a smaller topic that they could write about. Ask children to draw a picture or use a few written words to tell what their topic might be. Then have them share and discuss their possible topics and explain why his or her topic would be a good one to write about.

Reaching All Learners

BELOW LEVEL	ADVANCED	ENGLISH LANGUAGE LEARNERS
Allow children to work in pairs to generate topics. Monitor their discussion as you cultivate their strengths and guide them through the process of narrowing an idea.	Have children turn their topics into a story or other work. Remind them that they can use drawings, pictures from magazines, or even objects to help "tell" their stories.	Check to see that children understand the meaning of *big, small,* and *smaller.* Show three classroom objects of varying sizes. Point to the largest as you say: **big**. Have children echo as they point to the item. Repeat with *small* and *smaller*. Continue with additional classroom items.

© Harcourt

LESSON 3
Choosing Details

OBJECTIVES
- To recognize details
- To understand the importance of details in writing
- To use details to describe an object or a person
- To write details

Oral Warm-Up Display the covers of three or four books children have read. Remind children that they have read all of the books by giving a one- or two-sentence recap of each one. Then point to the books and say:

> **Right at this moment, I am thinking about one of these books. Can you tell me which book I am thinking of?**

Each time a child names one of the books say: **That might be the book I am thinking of. But do you know for sure?** After several tries that lead to the same response from you, it should become clear to children that there is no way to know for sure which book you are thinking of. Continue by asking: **How can I let you know which book I am thinking of without touching it or telling you its name?** Elicit from children that they would need to know more things about the book in order to know the answer. Say: **I am going to give you clues about my book to see if that helps.** Start by slowly offering a few details about the book, such as the color or size of its cover or something about the content or characters. Continue until children guess correctly. Then say: **Well, it seems the clues help you know what I am thinking.**

Teach/Model Explain that each clue that was given in the Oral Warm-Up is a *detail*, a little piece of information about the book or object. Add that good writers also tell interesting bits of information about a topic and that these details are what make their writing interesting.

> You can sometimes think of details by closing your eyes and painting a picture in your mind. Suppose you want to write about a trip to the bakery. Close your eyes. Think about the bakery. What do you see in the bakery? How does it smell? What do you hear? Who else is there? What are people doing?

Reaching All Learners

BELOW LEVEL	ADVANCED	ENGLISH LANGUAGE LEARNERS
Closely guide children through their thoughts about a bakery. If they have difficulty visualizing, ask questions that are even more specific. Encourage children to tell you about problems they have as they try to visualize. Help them visualize one small part of the scene at a time.	Have children write a poem to tell what they have visualized about the bakery. Invite them to tell the class what they have visualized—and then to read the poem. Point out the details in the visualization and how they came through in the poem.	Check to see that children understand what you mean when you say, "painting a picture in your mind." Have children spend a few seconds looking at a pen. Then have them close their eyes and tell you about the pen. Explain that when children's eyes are closed and they are telling you about the pen they are telling you about the "picture painted in their minds."

© Harcourt

Pause for responses as you ask each question. Tell children that each of their answers is another step in painting a complete picture of the bakery in your mind.

Guided Practice Tell children that good writers tell interesting, important details about a topic. Explain that, as young writers, they should practice thinking about details to put in their writing. Say:

> **Suppose you were writing about a favorite place in your neighborhood or community. The place can be someone's backyard, a movie theater, a ball field, a room in your home, even school, or a part of this school that you like best.**

Tell children to think of something special that happened in this place. Have them close their eyes and paint a picture of the place in their minds. Explain that you are going to ask questions to help them paint clear pictures. Ask:

> **What exactly are you looking at? What do you see ahead of you? What do you see if you turn around? What do you see to the side? What can you touch? Are you warm? Are you cool? Is there a window nearby? What do you see through the window? Are there any special smells?**

Have children open their eyes and think about the place they have pictured. Continue immediately to the Independent Writing Practice.

Independent Writing Practice Where Am I?: Provide paper and crayons. Have children draw their favorite places. As they begin to draw, remind children to keep their eyes closed and think about the answers to the questions they gave about their favorite places. Encourage children to add more details beyond those that answered your questions. Have children write or dictate a caption or sentence for their pictures when they are completed.

> **SHARING AND DISCUSSING**
>
> Have children show and discuss their drawings. Ask them to tell what they saw in their minds—and how they put this on paper.

HANDS ON ACTIVITY: WORTH A THOUSAND WORDS

Materials: paper, tape, and crayons

Directions:

1. Invite groups to make mini-murals on butcher paper (or sheets of regular-sized paper taped together). Have group members choose (out of earshot of other groups) a street in the neighborhood or community to depict in the mural. Then have members discuss the details to include for each building or feature of the street as well as for the street as a whole.

2. After the murals are completed, invite other groups to identify the street and all the places on it. Have children discuss the features that helped them recognize each place on the street. Explain that features are details that make the drawings more interesting and help others "see" the whole picture, just as details help a reader "see" what a writer has written.

© Harcourt

LESSON 4
Choosing the Best Details

OBJECTIVES
- To identify interesting, relevant details
- To distinguish between relevant and irrelevant details
- To write interesting, relevant details

Oral Warm-Up Remind children that good writers use interesting details to tell about their topics. Then say:

I'm going to tell you two stories about going to the supermarket. When I finish, I want you to tell me which story you like better. Here's the first story: *I like to go to the market. There are lots of things there. I did my homework last night.*

Now, here's the second story: *I like to go to the market. I stop and look at all the brightly colored magazines and books. I smell the delicious smell of fresh bread in the bakery. I push the cart and listen to the sound of the wheels squeak. I feel the prickly skin of pineapples and the slippery outsides of grapefruit and oranges.*

Ask children which story they like better and why. Guide children to see that the second story is more enjoyable because it is filled with interesting details that tell about the topic. In the first story, though, the details are not interesting and one of them is about homework, which has nothing to do with a trip to the market.

Teach/Model Tell children that each detail in a piece of writing should be interesting to hear or read and should tell more about the topic. Place a pencil box on a desk or table at the front of the room. In front of the box, place pens, pencils, crayons, and markers. Additionally, provide several items of similar size that are <u>not</u> used for drawing, such as a comb, some keys, and so on.

Model **This is my drawing box. I want to put in it ONLY things for drawing. I'll put a pencil in the box because I use a pencil for drawing.**

Place a pencil in the box. Then say: **What else should I put into the box?** Have a volunteer come forward, select another item, and tell whether it is used for drawing. If the object is used for drawing, have the volunteer put it into the box. Have volunteers take turns as you hand them various objects. At the end of the activity, point out that the drawing box is like a *topic.* Everything that goes into a piece of writing should be about the topic, just as everything that goes into the drawing box should be for drawing.

HANDS ON ACTIVITY: FINDING PIECES THAT FIT

Materials: index cards, magazine pictures or paper, and a pen

Directions:

1. Place a sketch or picture of each of the following on an index card: shell, sand, ocean, crab, sun, snowman, mountain, bear. Turn the index cards face down.

2. Tell children their topic is *A Day at the Beach.* Have a volunteer flip a card, show the picture to the class, and tell if the picture shows something about a day at the

beach. Encourage the child to explain the answer and say either: "This is a detail about a day at the beach" or "This is <u>not</u> a detail about a day at the beach."

3. After all the cards have been shown and discussed, invite another volunteer to pick up all the day-at-the-beach pictures and use them to tell an interesting story.

Complete the activity by reinforcing the idea that the details a writer uses should be interesting and should tell more about the topic.

Guided Practice   Remind children that good writers include interesting details that tell more about the topic. Then say: **I'm taking all of you on a picnic. What do I need? Let's see. I need some apples.** Write the word *apple* on the board. Then ask the whole class to recite along with you:

> **We're going on a picnic. We're taking some apples. What else do we need?**

Choose a volunteer to suggest something to take along. Write the suggestion on the board, and have children repeat it as you read it aloud. Then have the class say along with you: **We're going on a picnic. We're taking some apples and _____. What else do we need?** Choose a volunteer, write his or her suggestion on the board, and continue in the same way until each child has had an opportunity to participate. Periodically, review the list on the board, asking children if these details about your picnic are interesting and if they all belong on a picnic.

Independent Writing Practice   **Tell Me More:** Ask children to pick their favorite item from the list on the board. Then have them use words and pictures to put down on paper at least three details about that item. (For example, for apples, they might write the words *red, shiny,* and *big* and draw pictures to suggest the color, shape, and taste of apples.) When children finish, have them share their details, so the group will know as much as possible about the items they are taking on the picnic.

⭐ **Extra Practice**

Into a shoebox, place several pictures that might serve as story starters—a snowy day, a school bus traveling along a road, a young puppy, or whatever might be of interest to children. Have children take turns choosing a picture, writing a topic that goes with it, and drawing pictures to show details that would fit with it.

Reaching All Learners

BELOW LEVEL

Prepare children for the Independent Writing Practice by showing them objects, one by one, and having them suggest other objects or qualities that relate to each of them. (For example, if you show a pencil, children might suggest the word *yellow*, a picture of an eraser, or a pencil mark on a piece of paper.

ADVANCED

Suggest that children working at an advanced level create a story about what might happen on this picnic. Encourage them to include as many of the listed details as possible in the events of their stories. Children can tell their stories to the class.

ENGLISH LANGUAGE LEARNERS

Children might have difficulty coming up with words naming things associated with a picnic. Pair students with more proficient English speakers. Then have the pairs discuss what might be done on a picnic—the places that might be visited, the foods that might be eaten, and the activities that might be done. Pairs can make special Picnic Dictionaries, listing words they use in their discussions. Remind children to consult these dictionaries as they work on the Independent Writing activity.

© Harcourt

LESSON 5
Is Anything Missing?

OBJECTIVES
- To distinguish between complete and incomplete content
- To understand the importance of making content complete
- To determine how to make content complete
- To write complete content

Oral Warm-Up Cut out several clouds of varying sizes from a sheet of colored construction paper. Then display the cover of a Big Book that the children have not yet seen. Obscure large portions of the cover with the clouds so children cannot recognize what is on the Big Book cover. Then ask: **Can you see what the cover of this book shows?** After children respond that they can't, ask: **Why not?** Guide children to recognize that, because so much of the picture is covered, it is impossible to know what is on it. Then, one by one, remove the clouds, each time asking: **Can you tell what the picture is now?** Continue until children have identified the picture.

Explain that it is important to see a whole picture in order to understand what it shows and what it is about. Tell children that the same thing is true about writing. A writer must give enough information for the reader to know what a story or other piece of writing is about.

Teach/Model Remind children that good writers make ideas clear so the reader can see and understand. Make a sentence strip for each of the sentences in the story below. Then tell the story and, afterwards, post the sentence strips and read the entire story again. Say:

> **I'm going to tell you a story. Make pictures in your mind as you listen.** *Liam went home after school. He was tired. He fell asleep before he did his homework. He turned in his homework the next day.*

Help children recognize that this story is not clear because it is missing important information. Ask children what else they want to know—and why. Guide children to recognize that the story, as it is now, does not explain *how* or *when* Liam did his homework. Summarize by saying: **The writer left out some important information. It was as if there were clouds covering those parts of the story. The writer has to take away the clouds by writing clear, complete information.**

HANDS ON ACTIVITY: I CAN SEE CLEARLY NOW

Materials: construction paper, crayons, and markers

Directions:

1. Have small groups work out of earshot of one another to discuss ideas for a short story. When a group has decided on a story, each group member should draw a picture that shows an important part of it. Children should then lay out their pictures and number them in story order.

2. Invite a group to line up, holding their pictures in story order. The child with a detail from the middle (the "silent" member) should cover his or her drawing with a cloud from the Oral Warm-Up. The other group members should show their pictures and begin telling the story in order. The "silent" member should pantomime zipping his or her lips rather than telling that part of the story.

3. Have the class discuss how the missing part makes the story incomplete. Then have the "silent" group member remove the cloud to show the picture and reveal the missing detail. Continue with other groups.

© Harcourt

Ask children what kinds of information they might add to make the story more complete. Create new sentence strips with that information, and retell the story with the added details. Be sure to read the revised story slowly, tracking the words on the sentence strips as you read them.

Guided Practice   **Clarifying Content:** Remind children that good writers make their writing clear and complete. Write each of the following stories on the board. Tell children that you will ask them which story is clear and complete and which story is not. Track the print with your finger as you read each story aloud.

> **1**
> The frog saw a friend.
> The friend was on the other side of the pond.
> The frog jumped across the pond.
> It landed near its friend.

> **2**
> The cat ran.
> It fell in the yard.
> The cat was in the house.

Guide children to identify Story 1 as being better because it has more information about what happened. Help them recognize that Story 2 is <u>not</u> clear because it is missing important details. Have children suggest details that would make Story 2 clear, helping them see that it needs information about what happened to the cat. Share the pen with volunteers, having them suggest information that could be added to make Story 2 more complete.

Wrap up by reminding children that writers need to include enough information to make what they are writing clear to the reader.

Independent Writing Practice   Have children draw a picture and write a sentence that would make Story 2 clear for the reader. Tell them to begin by thinking about what else the reader needs to know. Then they should think about what to put on paper to make that information clear for a reader. Explain that this will take away the cloud over the story and make the story complete.

SHARING AND DISCUSSING

Have children share the pictures and sentences they wrote during the Independent Writing Practice. Invite them to discuss what they have learned about the importance of making information clear when they write.

Reaching All Learners

BELOW LEVEL	**ADVANCED**	**ENGLISH LANGUAGE LEARNERS**
Allow children to work in pairs to discuss what is missing in Story 2. Monitor their discussion, prompting them with questions such as, "How did the cat fall?" and "What happened when it fell?"	Have children turn Story 2 into a short skit. Tell them to include details that provide the information that would make the story clear for the audience.	Children might not know the words to describe the cat's actions. Have them work with more proficient English speakers to make a list of words telling what a cat might do in a yard and how a cat might get into a house. Children can use the list as a reference when they do the Independent Writing Practice.

© Harcourt

Writer's Companion • UNIT 1
Lesson 5 *Is Anything Missing?*

LESSON 6
Sentences

OBJECTIVES

- To understand the connection between a sentence and a complete thought
- To identify the naming part, telling part, and end mark of a sentence
- To recognize complete sentences
- To write complete sentences

Oral Warm-Up Tell children that they are going to play a game. Then say: **Let's play a sentence game. A sentence tells a complete thought. Here's a sentence:** *We hop.* **Let's act out this sentence.** *We hop.* Have children join you in hopping. Following the same pattern, repeat with different sentences, such as *We clap. We smile. We frown.* Then ask: **What if I say just the word** *we?* **Can you act out the word** *we?* Guide children to recognize that they cannot act out the word *we* because it does not tell a complete thought. It is not a sentence.

Teach/Model Explain to children that a sentence is a group of words that tells a complete thought. Then say: **A sentence has two parts. It has a naming part and a telling part.** Write the following sentence on the board or on chart paper:

> We hop.

Read the sentence aloud, tracking the print with your finger. Then point to the word *We* and say: **The word** *We* **is the naming part of the sentence. It tells who the sentence is about.** Point to the word *hop* and say: **The word** *hop* **is the telling part of the sentence. It tells what** *We* **do.** Point to the period and say: **Each sentence has an end mark. This period is the end mark for the sentence.**

Next, write the following sentence from *All That Corn* on the board: *The corn is in cans.* Read the sentence aloud, tracking the words with your finger. Then, as you point to relevant parts of the sentence, model the thought processes involved in determining if a group of words is a sentence.

Model I know a group of words must tell a complete thought to be a sentence. Let's see. I'll read the group of words again: *The corn is in cans.* This group of words does tell a complete thought. It tells me where the corn is. Here is the naming part: *The corn.* And I see a telling part: *is in cans.* I see that a sentence can have more than one word in the naming part. It also can have more than one word in the telling part.

HANDS ON ACTIVITY: FRIEND MOBILE

Materials: manila paper, hole-puncher, clothes hangers, yarn, pencils, crayons, and paper strips reading "My friend can ___"

Directions:

1. Pre-punch holes in the manila paper and sentence strips. Give each child a piece of manila paper, a sentence strip, and two long pieces of yarn. Have children draw a picture of a friend on the manila paper.

2. Tell children to write a word on the strip that tells something that their friend likes to do.

3. Help children use yarn to hang the pictures and word strips from the hangers. Invite children to name the friend and share their pictures and writing. Display the friend mobiles in the classroom.

Reread the entire sentence: *The corn is in cans.* Then say: **I know a sentence must have an end mark.** Point to relevant parts of the sentence as you say: **I see the end mark. It is a period. This group of words tells a complete thought. It has a** *naming part.* **It has a** *telling part.* **And it has an** *end mark.* **It is a complete sentence.**

Extra Practice

Read to children from favorite classroom books. Pause periodically to reread a sentence and have children tell you the *naming part, telling part,* and *end mark* of that sentence.

Guided Practice   Remind children that a sentence is a group of words that tells a complete thought. Write each of the following words and groups of words on separate sentence strips. Have children explain why they think each word or group of words is or is not a sentence. With each correct response, reinforce that a sentence tells a complete thought. It has a naming part, a telling part, and an end mark.

Linda runs.   We play with the ball.
The dog and cat   goes home
Dad makes dinner.   Mom

Tell children that the class will play a new sentence game called *Let's Get Together.* On poster board, write two-word sentences such as the following, making certain that subjects and verbs agree interchangeably: *I do. You help. We do. I hop. You run.* Display the poster board, and read the sentences aloud. Point out the naming part, telling part, and end mark of each sentence.

Cut each sentence into three pieces, noun, verb, and period. Turn the pieces face down and mix them up. Have each child choose a card. Then tell children to walk around the room and find two other children whose cards will help them be part of a sentence. Explain that they will form groups of three with a naming part, a telling part, and an end mark. After children have formed groups, have each group show its three cards. Guide them in saying about each group of words: **I'm the naming part. I'm the telling part. I'm the end mark.** Then have group members read aloud the sentence and say: **We make a complete thought. We are a sentence.**

Independent Writing Practice   **Writing Sentences:** Have children write the sentence their group formed. Provide yellow, blue, and pink highlighters. Tell children to highlight the *naming part* in yellow, the *telling part* in blue, and the *end mark* in pink.

Reaching All Learners

BELOW LEVEL	ADVANCED	ENGLISH LANGUAGE LEARNERS
Before children highlight the parts of their sentence in the Independent Writing Practice, help them point out the naming part, telling part, and end mark. Monitor as they highlight.	Have children create a short book with the title *Things I Like.* Tell them to draw a picture and write a sentence or two on each page to tell about things they like. Have them check their book pages and identify any complete sentences they have made.	Pair children with more proficient English speakers for the Independent Writing Practice. Have pairs talk about the words in the sentence their group made so the child has a solid grasp of the meaning of each word before writing the sentence.

© Harcourt

LESSON 1
Great Beginnings

OBJECTIVES

- To understand the importance of a good beginning
- To recognize good beginnings
- To write good beginnings

Oral Warm-Up   Tell children that you are going to tell them about two different places. Say:

> **What if there are two roads in front of you? The first road has nothing on it. There are no trees, people, or even cars nearby. On the second road, you see a circus clown. You see jugglers. You smell popcorn. Which road would you want to go on? Why?**

After listening to children's responses, point out that writing can be like the two roads. Say: **Some writing can begin in a dull or boring way, like the empty road. Other writing might begin with something interesting or exciting, like the road with the clown and the jugglers. A writer's job is to begin with something exciting and interesting, so the reader will want to read more.**

Ask children to recall a favorite movie and have them share the beginning. Invite them to discuss why the opening made them want to keep watching.

Teach/Model   Explain that a writer often "grabs" the reader's interest by using colorful language, or words that tell how things look, sound, smell, taste, and feel.

Read aloud pages 12–13 of *Dan's Pet*. Have children listen for words that describe how the chick looks, sounds, and feels. Ask children how the writer lets them know that the baby chick feels soft. Then ask children whether this makes a good beginning for a story and why.

Write the following sentences on the board: *There was a chick. There was a boy. He had the chick.* Read the sentences aloud, tracking the words with your finger as you read. Invite children to discuss why the opening of *Dan's Pet* is better than the opening you just read. If necessary, reread the opening of *Dan's Pet,* and have children tell you what they like about it.

HANDS ON ACTIVITY: TO BEGIN WITH

Materials: classroom library books

Directions:

1. Have each child look through classroom library books for a book with a great beginning.
2. Encourage children to look for things in the beginning that they can see, hear, smell, taste, or feel in their imaginations.
3. Have children share their great beginnings and sensory findings with the class.

© Harcourt

Guided Practice   Remind children that good writers write beginnings that make readers want to read on. Then tell children they will write a beginning for a new story. Say:

> **I know I can write a great beginning by telling how things look, sound, smell, taste, and feel. I want to write a story about pets.**

Write the following sentences on the board:

> I have a pet. He is a lot of fun. We do things together.

Read the sentences aloud, tracking the words with a finger. Say:

> **I could begin a pet story with these sentences:** *I have a pet. He is a lot of fun. We do things together.* **But when I read these sentences, they're not very interesting. I don't think they will make someone want to read on. I want to write a beginning that's more interesting than that. I think I'll get ideas by looking at pictures of pets.**

Display several pictures of pets in action—dogs, cats, parakeets, etc. Then write a sentence such as the following to describe one of the pictures: *The black dog chased a green ball.* Read the sentence aloud, tracking with your finger as you read. Then have children suggest good beginning sentences about the other pet pictures. Encourage and compliment children on their use of language as they speak. If they need help, remind children to think about what different pets might do and how they might look, sound, smell, and feel.

Independent Writing Practice   **Sense Words:** Keep the pet pictures displayed. Have each child settle on one picture and write a story beginning for it on another sheet of paper. Remind children to include things they might see, hear, smell, or feel.

SHARING AND DISCUSSING

Have children discuss the beginnings they created during the Independent Writing Practice. Talk about how some children made their beginnings interesting by using seeing, hearing, smelling, tasting, and feeling words.

Reaching All Learners

Below On-level Advanced ELL

BELOW LEVEL	**ADVANCED**	**ENGLISH LANGUAGE LEARNERS**
Before children begin the Independent Writing Practice, have them share their ideas with you. Ask why the reader will want to read on. Guide children in helping readers know how things look, sound, smell, and feel.	Have children add more sentences to the beginning created during the Independent Writing Practice. Challenge them to include at least three senses in their great beginnings.	English language learners may not be familiar with all of the sensory vocabulary used during the lesson. Make certain they understand the meaning of: *see, hear, smell, taste,* and *feel.* Take children on a classroom walk, pointing out how things look, sound, smell, taste, and feel. Reinforce as you discuss each by saying: **see**, **hear**, **smell**, **taste**, or **feel**.

LESSON 2
Strong Middles

OBJECTIVES
- To understand the importance of writing a strong middle
- To recognize strong organization in the middle of a piece of writing
- To write a strong middle

Oral Warm-Up Tell children to listen as you read aloud and pantomime the following actions. Say:

Let's imagine I am making a grilled cheese sandwich. I start with two pieces of bread. I melt some butter in a pan and grill the bread. Then I eat the sandwich. Does that sound delicious? Did I do a good job?

Guide children to recognize that what you did was incomplete. Encourage them to suggest steps that you left out, recording children's responses on the board in separate phrases, such as *get some cheese, put cheese between the slices of bread,* and *grill the cheese sandwich on both sides.* Guide children to conclude that the way you cooked the grilled cheese sandwich made no sense because it was missing most of the middle steps, even adding the cheese!

With children's help, create a correct recipe for the grilled cheese sandwich. Begin by writing and reading aloud the first step: **First, I take two slices of bread.** Have volunteers dictate the remaining steps in order. Prompt children with time-order questions such as: **What do I do next? Then what do I do?** When the recipe is completed, make certain children understand that a recipe cannot work unless all of the steps are included and that they are followed in an order that makes sense.

Teach/Model Explain that, in many ways, a story is like a sandwich: All the parts—a beginning, middle, and an ending—must be there to make a story work. And they must be in an order that makes sense. Remind children that they have already learned about great beginnings. Now they will work with strong, interesting middles that keep a story moving.

Tell children that some story middles are written in time order. Turn to *Boots for Beth* and tell children you will read the middle of the story. Read aloud pages 38–47. When you are done, encourage children to summarize the events of the story middle.

HANDS ON ACTIVITY: IN THE MIDDLE

Materials: For each small group of five, one strip of paper per child, with one of the following sentences on each strip: *I needed new shoes. We went to the store. I tried on two pairs that I liked. One fit perfectly. I wore them home that day.*

Directions:
1. Help children read the sentences in random order.
2. Have children work together to arrange the sentences in story order.
3. When they are done, have each group read the story aloud. Encourage children to see if all groups came up with the same order.

Guided Practice   Write the following two sentences on the board, leaving room for several sentences between them.

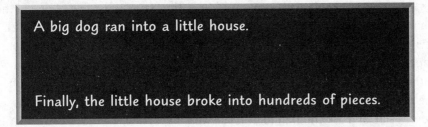

A big dog ran into a little house.

Finally, the little house broke into hundreds of pieces.

Point to and read each sentence aloud. Ask what is wrong with the story.

Elicit that there is no middle, so we don't know what happened or why the house broke apart into hundreds of pieces. Ask volunteers to think of middles that might work for this story. Praise at least some aspect of what each child offers. Look for and call special attention to story middles that are in time order, most especially those that use time-order words.

If children have trouble coming up with suitable middles, read the following:

> **A big dog ran into a little house. Soon, a bigger dog ran into the house. Then another and another and another ran in, too. Next, ten more big dogs ran into the house. After that came a hundred more. Finally, the little house broke into hundreds of pieces.**

Ask children to explain the middle in their own words. (More and more dogs ran into the little house until there were so many that the house broke apart.)

Independent Writing Practice   **Middles:** Tell children to write and illustrate their own middles for the dog story. Remind them to put the events in an order that makes sense.

SHARING AND DISCUSSING

Have children display and tell the whole story, including the sentences on the board. Encourage children to talk about each other's story middles, as well.

Reaching All Learners

BELOW LEVEL	**ADVANCED**	**ENGLISH LANGUAGE LEARNERS**
Talk with children about their middle story parts and how each step follows and connects with the beginning of the story. Have children discard or revise steps that do not fit with the beginning.	Challenge children to revise their strong middles with additional details and the words *first*, *next*, and *then*.	Guide English language learners in understanding the terms *beginning*, *middle*, and *ending*. Display books and magazines. Indicate the beginning, middle, and ending of each.

LESSON 3
Wonderful Endings

OBJECTIVES
- To understand the importance of a strong ending
- To recognize strong endings
- To write a strong ending

Oral Warm-Up Display two strips of ribbon. Tie a knot at the end of one of the ribbons, making the knot thick enough to prevent paperclips from sliding off. Invite a volunteer to slide paperclips onto the knotted ribbon and display the paper clips resting on the knot. Then have another volunteer hold the ribbon without the knot. Slide paperclips onto it and show how the paperclips fall off the ribbon. Repeat with another set of volunteers. Finally, show both ribbons side-by-side and ask children to describe what happened.

Guide children to explain that the paperclips stayed on the ribbon with the knot but fell off the ribbon without the knot. Point out that a good story ending is like a knot. It holds the parts of the story together.

Teach/Model Tell children that they have already learned about great beginnings and strong middles. Explain that they will now learn about wonderful endings—so they can finish their stories in an interesting way that makes sense. Return to *Boots for Beth* and read aloud pages 48–51. When you are done say:

> **What makes this a good story ending? First of all, the end of this story has a surprise. Beth now has a wonderful new pair of boots that her friends brought to her. A surprise is an excellent way to end a story. And this ending makes sense with everything that has already happened in the beginning and middle of the story. That makes it a good ending for a story.**

Explain there are more ways to write wonderful endings. On chart paper, write the heading *Endings*. Then begin a list with the word *surprise*. To the list, add: *a question, words someone says,* and *something funny.* Read aloud each entry on the list, tracking the words with your finger as you read. If you wish, have children echo your reading.

HANDS ON ACTIVITY: KNOT THE END

Materials: ribbon strips, crayons, manila paper with a hole in the middle, markers, and pencils

Directions:

1. Have small groups create Ending Knots of their own. For each group, provide a strip of ribbon and a piece of manila paper with a hole in the center. Tell children to make a knot at the end of the ribbon.

2. Have groups brainstorm the beginning and middle of a story about an animal that has an unusual adventure. Explain that they should agree on a wonderful ending for the story and draw a picture to show it. Tell children to write a sentence or two to tell about the picture.

3. Have children slide the paper with the ending onto the Ending Knot. Invite them to discuss the wonderful ending and explain why it is strong enough to stay on the Ending Knot without sliding off.

© Harcourt

Guided Practice   Remind children that good writers write wonderful endings that tie up a story in an interesting way that makes sense. Refer to the *Endings* chart as you review the kinds of endings discussed earlier. Then read aloud all of *Space Pup*. Ask: **What kind of ending does this book have?** Guide children to understand that *Space Pup* ends with a surprise. Ask why the ending is interesting. Then ask how the ending makes sense with the rest of the story. Guide children in recognizing that it makes sense that the pup would have been dreaming.

Explain that children will now think of wonderful endings for another story. Say:

> **After I tell the beginning and middle of my story, I'll ask you to take the Ending Knot and tell a wonderful ending. Here's my story:** *Oscar's dog got loose. It ran through the mud. It dashed through the leaves. Then it headed toward our house.*

Hand the Ending Knot to a child and invite the child to tell an ending to the story. After he or she has finished, compliment the child and have the child pass the Ending Knot to a volunteer who wants to tell a different ending. Pause to discuss each of the endings. Ask: **How is this ending interesting? How does this ending make sense with the rest of the story?**

Independent Writing Practice   **Endings:** Have children draw a picture and write sentences to illustrate the endings they just told for the story about Oscar's dog. If they wish to rethink their endings, remind children to refer to the *Endings* chart.

SHARING AND DISCUSSING

After the Independent Writing Practice, have children share their stories with the class. Invite children to explain how the ending ties up the story in an interesting way that makes sense.

Reaching All Learners

BELOW LEVEL	**ADVANCED**	**ENGLISH LANGUAGE LEARNERS**
Before children write the ending, ask them to discuss it with you. If necessary, guide the child in making it stronger, focusing on aspects such as whether the ending ties to the beginning and middle and whether the ending finishes the story in a way that makes sense.	After children have completed their stories, ask them to write two other possible endings. Have children share all three endings with the class and explain what they like about each one.	Meeting the vocabulary needs required to conceptualize a story ending may prove difficult for English language learners. Make certain children clearly understand the vocabulary that relates to the ending of a story, words such as *surprise, question,* and *funny.* Evaluate children's understanding by asking them to say a sentence for each word.

LESSON 4
Putting Things in Order

OBJECTIVES
- To recognize the importance of organization in writing
- To understand how to organize a piece of nonfiction writing
- To write an organized piece of nonfiction

Oral Warm-Up Explain that you are going to act out something. Then pantomime as you say:

> **I want to make a flower grow. I'll begin by digging a hole. Then I'll put a seed in the hole and cover it. At the end, I'll water the seed. What do you think will happen?**

Guide children to see that the seed probably will grow. Then guide children to understand that each step is necessary and that, if a step is skipped, a flower will not grow: **What would happen if I didn't dig a hole? What if I didn't put a seed in the hole? What if I didn't water the seed?**

Sum up by reminding children that, no matter what kind of plant a gardener wants to grow, he or she has to take care to follow certain steps.

Teach/Model Tell children that just as there are all kinds of plants and flowers, there are all kinds of writing. Say: **Not all writing is a story. Think of all the things people write. People write lists and letters. They write plays and poems. And, of course, they write about information.** Encourage children to suggest examples of these and any other kinds of writing they know. Then explain that all of these different kinds of writing have something in common: They all have beginnings, middles, and endings. Then write the following on the board.

> What looks like a baby fish but isn't a fish at all? Tadpoles look like baby fish. But they grow up into frogs. So when you see a baby fish, it could grow up to be a frog!

Read the paragraph aloud, tracking the words with your finger. Then say: **How is this paragraph organized? Let's start with the beginning. It starts with a question, which grabs my attention and makes me want to keep on reading. Then, there's the middle. It gives me facts and information about tadpoles. Finally, the last sentence sums up what I have learned.**

HANDS ON ACTIVITY: SEE THEM GROW!

Materials: lined paper, hole-punched tagboard, yarn, pencils, crayons, and glue

Directions:

1. Have groups create story trains. Tell children to brainstorm a story about how something grows up. Provide pictures of a small, medium-sized, and full-grown animal as a sample. Have children draw their growing-up pictures on each of three pieces of paper. Tell them to label the train cars *1* for the beginning, *2* for the middle, and *3* for the ending. Have groups draw a picture and write one or two sentences for each part of the story.

2. Tell children to glue each page to hole-punched tagboard. Have children use yarn to connect their story train cars in order.

© Harcourt

To reinforce the idea of organizing beginnings, middles, and endings, read the paragraph again, having volunteers come to the board and track each part—the beginning, middle, and ending—with their fingers as you read it aloud.

Guided Practice   Remind children that good writers write great beginnings, strong middles, and wonderful endings. Then work with children to identify those parts in *Where Do Frogs Come From?* Begin by pointing to the title page and first page and sharing the words and pictures (pages 86–88) with the children. Ask: **Why is this a great beginning?** Guide children to see that the question on the title page grabs the readers' attention and the first page starts readers off with the beginning of an answer.

Then read pages 89–95. As you read each page, have children sum up what they have learned about tadpoles so far. Ask: **What makes this a strong middle?** Guide children to understand that it gives the facts in an organized way by telling, in time order, how the tadpole grows.

Finally, read pages 96–98. Point out that the tadpole has now grown into a frog. Ask: **What is the frog doing at the end? What makes this a wonderful ending?** Guide children to recognize that pages 96–97 show that the tadpole has grown up into a frog; the last page shows what it will do for the rest of its life—chase bugs. Explain that in this way the ending wraps up all that has been going on in the previous pages.

Independent Writing Practice   **Story Order:** Tell children they will make their own book about where frogs come from. Provide five hole-punched pieces of paper for each child, labeled *1, 2, 3, 4,* and *5*. Have children draw a picture to show what happens in the beginning (*1*), middle (*2, 3,* and *4*), and ending (*5*) in the life of the frog. Then have them write one or two sentences to tell about each picture. When they have finished, have them use yarn to bind the pages together into a book.

Reaching All Learners

BELOW LEVEL	**ADVANCED**	**ENGLISH LANGUAGE LEARNERS**
Before children begin working with their graphic organizers, make certain they understand that Box 1 is for the beginning, Boxes 2, 3, and 4 are for the middle, and Box 5 is for the ending. Discuss children's proposed stories. Guide them in making certain that all the parts of the story connect to one another.	Challenge children to elaborate on the details of each story part. Have them add extra pages to their books as needed. Then have them make a colorful and interesting cover that will make readers want to pick up and read the book.	If possible, group English language learners with others who speak their primary language and are also proficient in English. Have children work together to create the story maps.

© Harcourt

LESSON 5
Building a Strong Story

OBJECTIVES
- To distinguish between strong and weak organization
- To understand how to write a strong beginning, middle, and ending
- To create an organized story

Oral Warm-Up Place three blocks in a row and tell children to imagine that these blocks are a road. Put a toy car on top of the first block and roll it across the three blocks. Then pick it up and place it on top of the first block again. Pause after each question as you ask: **What will happen if I pull the block from under the car? What will happen if I pull out the block in the middle? What will happen if I pull out the block at the end?**

Guide children to understand that, if blocks are missing, the car will not be able to go from the beginning to the end of the road; it might even fall. Sum up by explaining that the blocks are like a story and that the car is like the reader trying to get to the ending. If part of the story is missing, the reader cannot get to the ending.

Teach/Model Make certain children understand that the car they saw earlier is like a reader and the road is like a story. Say: **If the story is missing a great beginning, a strong middle, or a wonderful ending, the reader will not be able to make it from the beginning to the ending of the story.** Explain that a writer can make a smooth road for a reader by writing strong beginnings, middles, and endings.

On the board, draw a story map made up of three boxes in a row. Say:

> Help me begin a story about a foot race. We can start our race by thinking of an interesting beginning. Let's think of a beginning that will make the reader want to read on. Who will be in the race? Where will it take place?

Invite volunteers to offer ideas. Choose an idea and write one or two sentences in the first box. Follow the same procedure to get and record suggestions for a middle and ending to the story. Finish by saying:

HANDS ON ACTIVITY: ON THE ROAD AGAIN

Materials: toy cars, shoeboxes, tagboard, index cards, markers, and pencils

Directions:

1. Have groups of three draw a road on tagboard and draw lines to divide it into three parts. Draw a model on the board for children to follow. Ask children to write one of these numbers on each of three index cards: 1, 2, 3. Tell them to turn the index cards facedown in the box and mix them around.

2. Provide story starters on the board. Tell children to each draw a card from the box.

3. Explain that the child who draws 1 will tell the beginning of a story and place the car on the first part of the road. The child who draws 2 will tell the middle of the story and move the car to the middle of the road. The child who draws 3 will tell the ending and roll the card to the end of the road. If time allows, have children play the game several times.

© Harcourt

We now have good ideas. And we have put them in order. This helps the reader get from the beginning to the ending of our story.

Guided Practice Review the qualities of strong beginnings, middles, and endings. Read the following two stories below aloud as children listen carefully. Say: **One of these stories has a strong beginning, middle, and ending. The other does not. Which is strong and which is not? Who can explain why?** Before children answer and discuss the stories, have them listen to each story one more time. Guide children to see that the beginning of the first story does not grab the reader's attention, that the middle doesn't tell things in time order or make the actions clear, and that the ending doesn't tie up the story. Also guide them to see that, in contrast, the beginning of the second story gives specific information that gets the reader's attention, that the middle contains details told in time order, and that the ending paints a picture of how people felt and acted at the end.

SHARING AND DISCUSSING

Have children show their pictures and read aloud their sentences. Invite them to discuss which part of the story each child chose, (beginning, middle, or ending) based on their sentences and pictures.

STORY 1	STORY 2
Kids played ball. Her hit went very far. Kisha got a hit. Her team won. It was fun.	Our class played baseball today. Kisha got the best hit. The ball went "smack" and sailed to the field. Her team won by three runs. Everyone cheered and had fun.

Independent Writing Practice **Story Parts:** Review the events of the second version of the story. Then have children choose one part of the story—the beginning, the middle, or the ending. Tell them to draw a picture of that part of the story and write their own sentence describing what takes place.

Reaching All Learners

BELOW LEVEL	**ADVANCED**	**ENGLISH LANGUAGE LEARNERS**
With small groups, repeat the Oral Warm-Up. Make certain children understand the connection between the way a car travels and the way a reader needs a strong beginning, middle, and ending to get through a whole story.	Have children make believe they are teachers. Ask them to create posters with words and pictures to teach others how to write strong stories. Encourage children to tell about the beginning, middle, and ending of a strong story. Stress that the posters should be interesting and fun.	Make sure children have a strong grasp on all the vocabulary you have used, such as: *interesting, clear, read on, funny, tie, questions, see, hear, smell, taste,* and *feel*. Guide children to use each word in a sentence.

© Harcourt

LESSON 6
Capitalization

OBJECTIVES
- To recognize the importance of capitalization
- To capitalize special names, the word *I*, and the first word of a sentence

Oral Warm-Up Write the following paragraph on the board or chart paper and read it aloud.

> One day I went to give my friend's dog pat a pat on the head. "pat her again," my friend said. "My pet pat is shy. But she likes people to pat her and give her treats."

Say the word *pat* aloud, and ask volunteers to look for and circle the word each time it appears in the paragraph. Tell children that *pat* is a funny word because it can also be a name. Elicit from and review with children that a name always begins with a capital letter. Ask when else a word should begin with a capital letter (at the beginning of a sentence). Return to the paragraph and work with children to determine which of the circled *pats* needs a capital letter.

Teach/Model Explain that capital letters are important. Work with children to develop the rules below. Record the rules on chart paper (to begin a sentence; to write the word *I*; to begin a person's name; to begin the name of a day, month, street, city, or state).

Have children follow along as you read aloud page 113 of *Try Your Best*. As you read, point out the capitalized words, saying: **I see the word *Oh* at the beginning of the first sentence. The word *Oh* begins with a capital letter because it is the first word in the sentence. I also see the word *Ann*. The word *Ann* is not at the beginning of the sentence, but it is capitalized because it is a person's name. At the beginning of the next sentence, I see the word *I*. I know the word *I* must be a capital letter anywhere in a sentence.**

Reaching All Learners

BELOW LEVEL

Have children read aloud short classroom books. Have them point out the capital letters and explain why each one is capitalized.

ADVANCED

Invite children to write a story that includes all of the following: the word *I,* a day of the week, a month of the year, the name of a person, the name of a city, and the name of a state.

ENGLISH LANGUAGE LEARNERS

Guide English language learners in understanding that the word *I* is used to mean a person who is speaking or telling a story. Reinforce the capitalization of *I* in a variety of printed materials.

© Harcourt

Guided Practice Display a baseball cap or other type of cap. Tell children this is the capitalization cap. Explain they will use the cap as they show how well they know their capitalization rules. Display the chart with capitalization rules, and review the first rule. Ask a volunteer to come to the board to write an example. Hand the child the cap and say, "Here is the capitalization cap. Wear it while you write capitals." Invite additional volunteers to come to the board and write additional sentences for the rule. Tell each child to pass the cap to the next volunteer and say, "Here's the capitalization cap." Continue with the remaining rules.

Extra Practice

Have children copy the capitalization rules from the chart and write a sentence for each rule.

Next, take children on a classroom walk. Have them point out capital letters on posters, books, and other classroom items. Tell them to explain why each word is capitalized. Allow each child to wear the cap while telling the rule. Then have the child pass the cap to a volunteer who offers another example for the same rule.

Have children return to their seats. Write the following sentences on the board. Read each aloud. Guide children in finding the capitalization errors. Each time a child identifies an error, invite the child to come to the board, put on the capitalization cap, erase the lower-case letter, write the capital letter, and explain the capitalization rule that applies to the word.

> bob and i left the city.
> we drove to texas.
> we drove up maple street.
> it was a hot monday in july.

(Bob and I left the city. We drove to Texas. We drove up Maple Street. It was a hot Monday in July.)

Independent Writing Practice **Writing Sentences:** Provide simple classroom books that include a variety of words to exemplify the capitalization rules children have learned. Have pairs dictate several sentences from the books to one another. Tell children to be careful to use correct capitalization in their sentences. After the dictation, have children compare their sentences to the sentences in the books.

HANDS ON ACTIVITY: STICKY CAPITALS

Materials: sentence strips, sticky notes, and pencils

Directions:

1. On sentence strips, write an equal number of sentences with and without capitalization errors.

2. Distribute both sets of sentence strips—correct and incorrect—to small groups.

3. Tell children to sort the sentences into two piles, one with correct sentences and the other with sentences that include capitalization errors. Have children place a sticky note over each letter that should be capitalized. Tell them to write the capital letter on the sticky note.

© Harcourt

LESSON 1
Your Own Voice

OBJECTIVES

- To recognize and describe an individual's voice
- To write with a unique voice

Oral Warm-Up   Tell children to close their eyes, listen, and raise their hands as soon as they know who is talking. When children's eyes are closed say: **Today we are going to start with reading, then we will do some math, and then we will go to lunch.** By this time everyone's hands should be raised. Tell children to open their eyes. Then call on a volunteer to identify who was talking. Lead children to determine that they knew it was you not only by your voice but also by the words you spoke.

Teach/Model   Tell children that everyone's voice is different, and that a voice is more than what you sound like; it is also what you say and how you say it.

Tell children that you are going to speak in the make-believe voice of a butterfly, like one from the story *I Am a Butterfly*. Then, in a high-pitched, conceited tone say: **I can fly wherever I wish. Each time I settle down, it's on another beautiful flower. And wherever I go, I am the loveliest thing anyone sees. I am even more beautiful than the flowers.**

Ask: **What does the butterfly sound like? How do you feel about what the butterfly says?** Have children suggest words to describe the butterfly and write those words on the board.

HANDS ON ACTIVITY: HOW DOES IT FEEL?

Materials: manila paper, markers, crayons, and pencils

Directions:

1. Separate children to allow private workspace. Tell children to draw a butterfly they would like to see.
2. Then ask children to write a word or two to tell what the butterfly is like—gentle, proud, hard-working, and so on. The drawings can then be displayed in a Butterfly Gallery.

© Harcourt

Guided Practice   Explain that writers have a voice, too. They often speak through the characters they write about. Make it clear to children that the voice of the butterfly is really the voice of the writer—the one who put words into the butterfly's mouth.

Read aloud pp. 26–27 from *I Am a Butterfly*, using a "butterfly voice" to accentuate the key points. Pause after each page and ask: **What is the butterfly doing on this page? How does it feel about that? How do you know?**

When you have finished reading and discussing, have children adopt "butterfly voices" of their own and use them to describe other things a butterfly might see and do.

Independent Writing Practice   **Animal Voices:** Tell children they will write a page in the voice of a butterfly. Say: **As you get ready to write, think about the different things a butterfly might say and do.** Then have children use words, their butterfly drawings, or even pictures from magazines or newspapers to start off their pages. Have children share each of their butterfly's voices.

> ### Extra Practice
>
> Have children identify writer's voice in a variety of books and stories. Encourage them to notice what makes each piece of writing interesting and unique.

Reaching All Learners

BELOW LEVEL

Work with children individually to help them understand and find a voice for the Independent Writing Practice. Tell children to imagine that they are butterflies. Then ask the "butterflies" questions such as: *How do you feel about flying? What do you think about flowers? What can you do to show this?*

ADVANCED

Have children complete the pages they began in the Independent Writing Practice. Then invite them to share their pages with the class. Have children discuss each writer's voice, including what each butterfly does and what it is like.

ENGLISH LANGUAGE LEARNERS

The various meanings of the word *voice* may be particularly confusing for English language learners. Say: **When I talk, you hear my <u>voice</u>.** Then say: **When I write, my voice is what I think and feel.**

© Harcourt

LESSON 2
Voice and Feeling

OBJECTIVES
- To recognize feeling in voice
- To understand that a writer's voice should match the writer's feeling
- To write with a voice that matches feeling

Oral Warm-Up Ask children to think about their day in school. Say: **What if you are having a great day, a day when everything goes right? How would your face look? What would you say? How would your voice sound?** Have children make appropriate facial expressions, and invite volunteers to speak in a way that shows that they are pleased, excited, and happy about having a great day.

Then say: **But what if you had a terrible day, a day when everything went wrong? How would you look? How would your voice sound?** Again, encourage children to use their faces and voices to express the appropriate emotions. Sum up by explaining that the way people think and feel comes through in how they look, act, and speak.

Teach/Model Explain that a writer's voice, just like any person's voice, shows how the writer feels or wants a character to feel. Say: **When writers want their writing to sound happy, they will choose words to show that feeling. The same is true for sounding sad, upset, or silly.**

Tell children that you are going to look at some pictures together. Show a picture of someone feeling sad. Say: **How does this person seem to feel? How can you tell?** Encourage children to point out details in the picture that point to that feeling. Then ask: **Suppose I was writing about the person in this picture. What words could I use?** List children's suggestions on the board if necessary, prompt them with words such as *sad, blue, long face, tears,* and so on. Encourage children to explain how the words match the feeling of sadness in the picture.

Continue with other pictures, complimenting children for being able to identify moods and emotions and for suggesting words that express those emotions.

HANDS ON ACTIVITY: SHOW THE FEELING

Materials: manila paper, magazines or newspapers with pictures that can be cut out, scissors, and tape or glue

Directions:

1. For each group of three children, make a set of manila pages labeled *happy, sad,* and *silly*. Give a set of pages to each group.
2. Have children search magazines and newspapers for pictures illustrating each feeling. Have children tape or glue the pictures to the appropriate manila page.
3. Wrap up by having children discuss what they have found, explaining why each picture is a good example of a particular feeling.

Guided Practice Have children turn to page 41 of *Did You See Chip?* Point out the characters and read aloud the words, tracking them with your finger as you read. Say:

> I wonder how Kim feels right now. When I look at the picture, I can tell from the look on her face that she is sad. She is frowning and looks unhappy. When I read what she says, I understand this better because she misses her old home and wishes she had friends in her new one. That is the voice that comes through when she speaks.

Then have children turn to page 43. Tell them to look at the picture and listen as you read aloud Kim's words. Ask: **How do you think Kim feels now? How would you describe her voice?** Guide children to understand that Kim probably is upset and worried about Chip and that her voice probably has an excited tone to it.

SHARING AND DISCUSSING

Arrange for children to act out a page from the play, with children taking turns playing Kim and you taking the other parts.

Independent Writing Practice **Feelings:** Have children turn to page 51 of *Did You See Chip?* Read the page aloud, helping them summarize what is happening on the page. Then have children write a sentence about what Kim's voice is probably like now.

Reaching All Learners

BELOW LEVEL

To help children match voice to feelings, have them search through more sources for pictures showing various emotions. Have children match each picture with more appropriate emotions, such as *excited, scared, tired, bored,* and so on.

ADVANCED

Write the following sentence on the board: *I had the best birthday party ever!* Tell children to think of a list of words that express the emotions they would have after that party. Challenge them to turn the words into a poem about their feelings.

ENGLISH LANGUAGE LEARNERS

Reinforce vocabulary by pantomiming each of these words and then discussing them: *funny, silly, sad, strong, quiet, proud.* To assess children's understanding, have them pantomime along with you and use each word in a sentence.

LESSON 3
Choosing Your Voice

OBJECTIVES
- To develop an understanding of the connection between voice and purpose
- To write with a voice that matches a given purpose

Oral Warm-Up Display pictures of coats, hats, gloves, umbrellas, t-shirts, shorts, and other pieces of clothing. After each of the following questions, invite a child to pick out the clothing items you will need.

What if it is snowing outside? What do I need?
What if it is raining? What do I need?
What if it is very, very warm outside? What do I need?

Discuss the choices children make, guiding them to see that people try to match their clothing to the type of weather. Explain that, just as people match their clothes to the weather, writers match the voice they use to their reason for writing.

Teach/Model Remind children that people write for many different reasons. Sometimes they write to entertain or to persuade someone to do something. Sometimes they write to share information. Say: **I have two letters to write. One is to a friend who lives far away. I'd like to invite my friend to come visit for a few days. The other letter is to the mayor. I want to explain that we need more streetlights on our street. How will the letters be different?**

Talk with children about each letter and how a writer's voice should match the reason for writing. Determine with children that the letter to a friend may be funny and very friendly because a friend is someone we know very well. On the other hand, the mayor is someone we don't know, so that letter should sound polite and respectful. It should also have some important information to convince the mayor to add streetlights. Say: **So even though I am the person writing both letters, each letter will have to have its own voice.**

HANDS ON ACTIVITY: POST CARD FOR...

Materials: paper cut to resemble large postcards, pencils, crayons, and markers

Directions:
1. Tell children to imagine being at a faraway place, and to think of someone they know.
2. Have children write a "postcard" to that person, from that place. Emphasize that the writing should be in a voice that suits the person to whom they are writing.
3. Have children share their finished postcards.

Guided Practice   Remind children that writers use different voices for different kinds of writing. Say: **Let's think about some of the different kinds of letters I might write. What kind of voice should I use for each of them?**

Then discuss each of the following letter possibilities with the children:

- A letter to a sports company to complain that some equipment did not work
- A letter that thanks a grandparent for a gift you really enjoyed

Encourage children to think of why the letter is being written, to whom it is being written, and what might be the best voice to use.

Independent Writing Practice   Write a Letter: Have children write a letter to a friend. In their letters, children should describe the best thing they did this past summer. Encourage children to use their happiest, friendliest voice in the letter.

> **SHARING AND DISCUSSING**
>
> Have children share their work from the Independent Writing Practice. Help them to discuss the writer's voice used in each piece of writing.

Reaching All Learners

BELOW LEVEL	ADVANCED	ENGLISH LANGUAGE LEARNERS
Before children begin their letters for the Independent Writing Practice, help them make a list of the key points they would like to include in the letter.	Challenge children to write another letter in another voice that tells what they would like to do next summer.	For the Independent Writing Practice, pair English language learners with classmates who are more proficient in English. Have them brainstorm ideas and write the final letter together.

© Harcourt

Writer's Companion ● UNIT 3
Lesson 3 *Choosing Your Voice*

LESSON 4
Trying New Voices

OBJECTIVES

- To identify new and unusual voices in literature
- To write with a variety of voices

Oral Warm-Up Write this sentence on the board and read it aloud: *I want it now, please.* Then say the sentence several times, each time saying it as if you are in a different mood—politely, angrily, commandingly, whiningly, and so on. Point out that these words can seem very different when you hear them, depending on the kind of voice that is used.

Now write the sentence *It's time to walk the dog* on the board and have children say it politely, angrily, etc. as you did above. Tell children that emotions, or feelings, are also part of a writer's voice.

Teach/Model Explain that writers know that there are many voices that they can use. Say: **Writers look for new and interesting voices for their writing. The voices might express any one of a number of feelings. The feelings help us know who the characters are and make them more interesting.**

Direct children to *On the Way to the Pond*, on pages 90–102. Read aloud as children track the text. Ask children what they think the characters are like. Give children time to present their ideas about Herbert and Tess—what they are like, how they might sound, and so on. Then say: **Tess is a cat, so I think that her voice is going to sound something like "meeooow." I also think she always tries to know what she is doing but sometimes gets confused. So Tess's voice might sound a bit confused like this sometimes.**

Then read Tess's words on page 93, using an appropriate voice. Explain that using this new and different voice makes *On the Way to the Pond* fun for both the writer and the reader.

HANDS ON ACTIVITY: VOICES SCRAPBOOK

Materials: manila paper with punched holes, yarn, crayons and markers, and a mirror

Directions:

1. Give each child two pieces of paper with a hole about two-thirds of the way from the top of each side. Help children tie yarn through the holes to form a face mask.
2. Then ask children to think of different emotions—fear, worry, silliness, and so on. Tell them to try to make a face that would go with that emotion.

Encourage children to see what their faces look like in a mirror.

3. Help children use crayons and markers to make a mask for that emotion. When they have finished, organize a guessing game in which each child dons his or her mask and the other children try to guess the emotion.

© Harcourt

Guided Practice Explain that writers look for new and different voices to use. Say: **When writers use new voices, writers and readers get to see things in new and interesting ways.**

Remind children how you went about finding a voice for Tess when you were reading *On the Way to the Pond*. Then guide children to find a voice for Herbert. Use the following to prompt children's thinking: **Herbert is much bigger. What is his voice going to be like? Will it be deeper or higher than Tess's voice? And what is he like? Is he someone who plans things, the way Tess does? Does he get excited about things? Or is he more relaxed?** Give children time to think, discuss, and experiment. Then help them take turns reading Herbert's words on page 102, in their best "Herbert voices."

Independent Writing Practice **Character Voices:** Ask children to think of what Tess or Herbert might want do after they get home from the pond. Have children choose either Tess or Herbert and write some words telling what that character wants to do. Then have children read their words aloud. Remind children to use their Tess or Herbert voice for the speech.

SHARING AND DISCUSSING

Have children share their speeches from the Independent Writing Practice. Encourage children to read the speeches aloud to the group. Discuss how closely the children's versions of Tess and Herbert are to the voices in the story.

Reaching All Learners

BELOW LEVEL	**ADVANCED**	**ENGLISH LANGUAGE LEARNERS**
Before children write their speeches for the Independent Writing Practice, ask them to discuss their ideas with you. Help them match those ideas with the personality of each character.	Have children write and present short skits about another adventure Tess and Herbert might have.	Children may have difficulty thinking of appropriate words for the characters. Pair children with more proficient English speakers and have them generate lists of words that each character might use.

© Harcourt

LESSON 5
More New Voices

OBJECTIVES
- To develop a deeper understanding of writing in new ways
- To write in a variety of voices

Oral Warm-Up Tell children that you have another "voice" game for them to play. Say: **I'm a silly elephant. And I want to invite you to a party. What do I say?** Choose a volunteer to use a "silly elephant voice" to invite someone to a party. Continue with other made-up creatures and other volunteers, using such possibilities as a "big, big dog" who wants the mayor to build more dog parks, a "joking chimpanzee" who wants to thank someone for a great new joke, and so on.

Sum up by reminding children that finding and using new voices can be fun and can help writers write better stories.

Teach/Model Remind children that real people or characters in books have voices of their own. Direct children's attention to pages 116–117 of *Friends Forever*. Point out the first picture on page 116. Say:

Model Look at these two girls. They are friends. They are playing patty-cake. They are smiling and having a good time. If I wrote about this picture, I would use a happy voice that told readers just how good it was to be doing this with such a good friend.

Then talk with children about what the girls in the picture might be thinking and saying. Say: **I wonder if they are saying things like "This is fun!" What do you think the girls are like? Do you think that one is more serious than the other?** Encourage children to speculate about the people in the picture. List children's ideas on the board, complimenting children for recognizing the girls' feelings and for finding words to describe them.

HANDS ON ACTIVITY: THIS IS A FRIEND OF MINE

Materials: none

Directions:

1. Tell children to think of a friend of theirs—a classmate, a neighbor, or a relative, even an adult.
2. Ask children to imagine a conversation or some other situation in which they might be with their friend.
3. Then have children use their two index fingers as finger puppets, each "puppet" taking the part of one of the two friends. Have children use the puppets to speak in the voices of themselves and their friends.

Guided Practice Direct children to pages 118–119 for *Friends Forever*. Remind them that, as they read and look at the pictures, they are probably wondering about the people in the photographs. Say:

> **As I look, I wonder what each person is like. What does he or she like to do? What kind of personality does he or she have? What does this person do for fun? Where does this person go to school?**

Then point to the picture at the lower left of page 118. Say: **I can use what I've learned about voices to think about what these people are saying to each other. For example, I think the boy on the left is saying, "Hey, do you like to play basketball?" What do you think the other boy might say then?**

Continue in this way, helping children build a dialogue that might take place between the two boys in the photograph. Then continue with the photograph on page 119, guiding children to construct a conversation about the girl's injured arm.

SHARING AND DISCUSSING

Have children take turns performing their *Friends Forever* speeches. Encourage children to make the voices of the people in the photographs come through as they act out the speeches.

Independent Writing Practice **Draw What You Hear:** Tell children that, now, they will create their own dialogue or conversation for a picture in *Friends Forever*. Have children thumb through *Friends Forever* and choose a picture that interests them. Have them think about what the people in that picture might be saying to each other. Then, on a separate sheet of paper, have children write down something those people might say to each other. Encourage children to illustrate the page with drawings that help readers understand what is happening and what is being said.

© Harcourt

Reaching All Learners

BELOW LEVEL	**ADVANCED**	**ENGLISH LANGUAGE LEARNERS**
Help children get started in the Independent Writing Practice by brainstorming a list of things they and their friends like to talk about. Have the children consult that list as they write their speeches.	Have children extend their dialogues into small skits and plays that they can act out for the group.	Have children work with more proficient English speakers and make a list of words that children their age use everyday. Let children refer to these lists for this and other writing activities involving characters speaking.

LESSON 6
Writing Dialogue

OBJECTIVES

- To recognize dialogue in a story
- To understand the purpose of quotation marks
- To recognize words used to introduce a speaker's exact words
- To use quotation marks to indicate a speaker's exact words

Oral Warm-Up Ask a volunteer to tell you a sentence about their favorite part of the day. Write the child's exact words on the board. Then say:

I want to write your exact words in a story. I need to show the reader that these are exactly the words you said. I can do this by showing your exact words between special marks.

Write quotation marks at the beginning and end of the sentence. Then read the sentence aloud, tracking the words with your finger. Explain that, when a reader sees words between the special marks, the reader will know these are the exact words a speaker says.

Teach/Model Remind children that writers sometimes include the exact words a speaker says. Point to the example on the board as you show how the speaker's words are written between special marks. Then have children turn to pages 94–95 of *On the Way to the Pond*. Read the pages aloud, pointing out the special marks around the dialogue on page 95. Say:

Model **I see the first mark just before the word sit. Then I see the other after the word *umbrella*. This tells me that this sentence is spoken by one of the characters. Then I see the words *said Tess*. These tell me that the words *Sit under my umbrella* are spoken by Tess. Words like *said* help readers know who is speaking.**

Continue in this way with the rest of the page, pointing out the next set of words in quotation marks as well as the words spoken by Herbert. Sum up by explaining that whenever writers want to show the exact words of a speaker, they use these special marks and a word like *said, asked,* or *cried*.

HANDS ON ACTIVITY: HE SAID; SHE SAID

Materials: index cards and shoeboxes

Directions:

1. Write the words and punctuation in the following sentences on index cards, one word or punctuation mark to a card: *"Look in the box!" cried Pam. "Go home," said Juan. "Will you try?" asked Tran.*

2. Place all the cards that make up a sentence into one shoebox. Have groups arrange the cards correctly to show a sentence that includes the exact words a speaker says.

3. Allow all groups a chance to work with the sentence in each shoebox.

© Harcourt

Guided Practice Remind children that a speaker's exact words are written between special marks. Point out examples on the board. Direct children's attention to page 150 of *The Fox and the Stork*. Ask:

Do you see exact words that someone said? What are the words? (*Would you like to come to my house for dinner?*) **How do you know these are the exact words someone said?** (The words are inside special marks.) **Who said the words?** (Fox) **How can you tell?** (The words are followed by *Fox asked*.)

Have children continue through the story, pointing out the exact words of speakers as well as the special marks and words that help to show them who said what.

Independent Writing Practice **Writing Dialogue:** Have children write down part of a conversation or talk they had with someone else. Tell them to include the exact words that were spoken along with words like *said, cried,* and so on. When they have finished, have children share their conversations and explain how they marked the exact words that were said.

⭐ **Extra Practice**

Help children locate books containing classic tales and rhymes. Have children search them for speakers' exact words in quotation marks in yellow. Have children share their discoveries with the group.

Reaching All Learners

BELOW LEVEL

Guide children with Independent Writing Practice. Ask: **Did you write exact words someone says? Where do the speaker's words begin? What mark did you write there? Where do the speaker's words end? What mark did you write there? What word did you use to show who said the words?**

ADVANCED

Challenge children to write riddles. Provide this riddle as an example: *What did the bus driver say to the fish?* ("Which school do you go to?") Have children write additional riddles, using quotation marks in the answer to each. Invite children to share their riddles with the class.

ENGLISH LANGUAGE LEARNERS

Children might not be familiar with the many words that are used to introduce a speaker's exact words. Review those words with them, including *said, asked, cried,* and so on.

© Harcourt

LESSON 1
Words! Words! Words!

OBJECTIVES
- To recognize describing words
- To use describing words orally and in writing

Oral Warm-Up Tell children that words can be fun. Words can also help us tell about ourselves and the people we know. Say: **Suppose you wanted to describe me to someone. What would you say? What words would help that person know things about me?**

Encourage children to make suggestions, complimenting them for their ideas and putting the suggested words on a list on the board.

Teach/Model Remind children that they make their writing strong by using interesting words. Explain that these words help the reader see what the writer has in mind. These words also keep the reader interested in reading more of what the writer has written. Say: **Think about yourself and all the things that make you special or different from everyone else. Now think about all the different words that you would like someone to use to tell about you?** Then model the process of looking for interesting words to use in a description.

Model What words would I like someone to use about me? Let's see. Well, I like to ride my bike. I also like to play ball. That's because I really like sports. So someone could use the word *athletic* because I like sports and I am good at them. Let me write *athletic* on the board. What else would I like someone to say? Well, I work hard at things. So *hard worker* would be some other words that I could put on the list.

Now encourage children to think of words they would like someone to use to describe them. Write their suggested words on the board until you reach a list of a dozen or so. Review the list. Discuss with children how finding the right words can help people communicate their ideas about someone and keep readers and listeners interested.

Reaching All Learners

BELOW LEVEL
To help children think of words for the list, ask specific questions, such as the following: **What do you like to do? What do you look like? What are you good at?**

ADVANCED
Have pairs incorporate at least three words from the list into a poster that contains your name and a picture of you. Encourage children to choose the words that give the most accurate portrait of you and your personality.

ENGLISH LANGUAGE LEARNERS
Children may need help thinking of words with which to describe other people. Have them think of qualities they admire in other people. List those words on the board and encourage children to think of people who have those qualities. Ask children what other words could be used to describe those same people. Use these words to create a word list to which the children can refer.

© Harcourt

Writer's Companion • UNIT 4
Lesson 1 *Words! Words! Words!*

44

Guided Practice Take a ruler and attach a ribbon to it, telling children that this Word Wand will help them choose wonderful words to use. Pass the Word Wand to a volunteer, explaining that he or she is to take it, touch him- or herself gently on the shoulder, and say, "I pronounce myself *silly*. Arise Lord/Lady Silly and act silly." Tell the volunteer to then do something that everyone will think is silly. Add the word *silly* to the list of words on the board.

Continue with several more volunteers, having each child think of a word to describe him- or herself or to describe something he or she would like to be. Add children's words to the list on the board.

To wrap up, read aloud the words on the list, telling children that these are wonderful words to use when they are describing people.

Independent Writing Practice **Personality Words:** Give each child a piece of paper and tell children to fold their papers in half. Explain that on each side of the paper children will write a different sentence that tells something about themselves. For example, they can write "I am helpful" on one side and "I like computers" on the other side. Encourage children to use the two sides of the paper to tell people about different sides of their personalities.

> **SHARING AND DISCUSSING**
>
> Have children show their pictures and read their sentences aloud. Point out any new words they have used to describe their pictures. Add these words to the class list.

HANDS ON ACTIVITY: WONDERFUL WORD WHEELS

Materials: poster board, crayons, markers, and pencils

Directions:

1. Have pairs draw a wheel on poster board. Then guide them to divide the wheel into four parts.
2. Have each child in a pair choose a word from the *Word Wand List* and write it in one section of the word wheel.
3. Then have other child say the word and use it in an oral sentence.
4. Have children continue until they complete the wheel.

45

Writer's Companion • UNIT 4
Lesson 1 *Words! Words! Words!*

LESSON 2
Exact Nouns

OBJECTIVES
- To understand the importance of using exact nouns
- To identify exact nouns
- To write exact nouns

Oral Warm-Up Ask children to draw a picture of an animal. Then have them show their pictures and name the animals they drew. On the board, write the heading *Animals* and write names of the animals that children drew. Next, ask children to draw a picture of a turtle. Have all the children hold up their pictures. Say:

The first time, I asked you to draw an animal. And you drew different kinds of animals because you didn't know which animal I wanted you to draw. The second time, I told you exactly what I wanted you to draw. That time, everyone drew a turtle.

Teach/Model Tell children that an exact noun is a word that names something clearly and exactly. Explain that exact nouns help readers know precisely what a writer wants to say, which makes the writing easier to understand. Exact nouns also help make writing more interesting and fun to read. Tell children that this is why writers try to use exact words when they write. Model the process of choosing exact nouns.

Model I want to write a story about a toy someone gets for his birthday. I could write: *José tore open the box. It was a toy! He was so happy that he jumped up and down.* Let's see. Does the word *toy* paint a clear word picture for my readers? No, I don't think so. Readers could think of many different kinds of toys. They wouldn't know what kind of toy José got. What word could I use that is more exact than *toy*? Suppose I replace the word *toy* with *yo-yo.* Then my readers would know exactly what I meant.

HANDS ON ACTIVITY: EXACT NOUN WORD BOOKS

Materials: small and large index cards with a hole punched in each, pencils, and yarn

Directions:

1. Write these general nouns on the board: *pet, toy*. Tell small groups to choose one of the nouns and write it on a large index card.

2. Explain that children should then write an exact noun for their chosen word. Have them write their exact nouns on the smaller cards.

3. Help children tie the cards together with yarn. Have children keep their word books so they can add other exact words to each group.

© Harcourt

Guided Practice Remind children that an exact noun names something clearly and exactly. Point out the list of animals you wrote earlier. Then write a new heading on the board: *Food*. Ask children if this is an exact noun, guiding them to see that it is not. Then have children tell exact nouns they might use to replace the word *food*. Repeat with the heading *Clothing*.

⭐ **Extra Practice**

Label three shoeboxes with the following words: *Animals, Food, Clothing*. Cut out pictures from old magazines to show specific examples related to the general nouns. Mix up the pictures and have children place each one in the correct box.

Animals	Food	Clothing
dog	apple	hat
bear	bread	coat
tiger	soup	dress
fish	cookie	gloves
lion	peanut	shirt
turtle	egg	pants

Work with children to identify exact nouns on the chart that can be narrowed even further, such as *fish* (*shark, tuna, cod*), *pants* (*shorts, jeans, exercise*), or *soup* (*tomato, vegetable, alphabet*).

Independent Writing Practice **Specific Words:** Write these general nouns on the board: *tools, buildings*. Read them aloud and discuss the meaning of each one. Tell children to choose one of the general nouns. Then have them write at least three more exact nouns to replace that noun. Have children draw a picture to illustrate each exact noun.

Reaching All Learners

BELOW LEVEL	ADVANCED	ENGLISH LANGUAGE LEARNERS
After children write their exact nouns in the Independent Writing Practice, review the nouns with them, making certain that each exact noun relates to the general noun.	Have pairs create riddles that include a general noun and clues in the question. Tell children the answer must be an exact noun. Have them write the question on one side of an index card and the answer on the other.	Review the general and exact nouns from the chart. Invite children to add other exact nouns in English and in their native language.

LESSON 3
Exact Verbs

OBJECTIVES
- To understand the importance of using exact verbs
- To identify exact verbs
- To write exact verbs

Oral Warm-Up Write this sentence on the board and read it aloud: *Mia looked*. Then say:

> The word *looked* is not clear in this sentence. It is a verb, a word that tells about an action. But it does not paint a clear word picture for the reader. What else could I write? What about *Mia stared* or *Mia peeked*? In what ways do the verbs *stared* and *peeked* paint clearer word pictures for the reader?

Teach/Model Explain that an exact verb tells about an action clearly and exactly. Tell children that exact verbs help writers tell readers precisely what is happening. That is why writers use exact verbs whenever they can. Model the process of choosing exact verbs.

> **Model** I am writing a story about a squirrel. Suppose I want to write about how a squirrel went across a street. The word *went* doesn't paint a clear picture for my readers. What else could I write? What if I write: *The squirrel ran across the street*? That tells readers that the squirrel moved quickly. But is there a better, more exact word? What if I write *dashed*? or *hopped*? These verbs are even more exact. They tell more about how the squirrel moved and how fast it went. I think I'll write: *The squirrel dashed across the street*. Then my readers will get a clearer picture of what I mean.

On the board or chart paper, begin a verb list with the heading *go*. Ask children to think of how people and animals go places. Begin a list of exact verbs with *dash*. Then invite children to offer additional exact verbs to replace the general verb *go* (examples: *scampered, trotted, leaped*). After you write the list, ask children to tell how each verb paints a different word picture in their minds.

Sum up by discussing with children how exact verbs help writers communicate their ideas.

HANDS ON ACTIVITY: EXACT VERB PICTURES

Materials: old magazines, index cards, paste or tape, and pencils

Directions:

1. Form pairs. With children's help, on the board write a list of exact verbs to replace go. Then have pairs cut out magazine pictures that show people and animals moving/going. Tell children to paste or tape each picture to an index card.

2. Have pairs show a picture and then pantomime the action. Invite the rest of the class to guess the word written on the other side of the card.

© Harcourt

Guided Practice   Remind children that an exact verb tells an action in an exact and clear way. Point out the list of exact verbs you wrote to replace *go*. Then add another heading: *says*. Ask children if *says* is an exact verb, guiding them to see that *says* does not give readers a mental picture of just how someone said something. Have children suggest exact verbs they might use in a story to replace the unclear verb *says*. Add their suggestions to the chart.

Extra Practice

Have children share their work from the Independent Writing Practice. Make a class list of verbs children used to replace *do*.

go	says
dash	yells
run	whispers
race	asks
crawl	shouts

Direct children's attention to the photo on page 85 of *At Home Around the World*. Say: **I could write:** *The girl goes up the path.* **But that sentence does not do a good job of telling the action in the picture. Why not?** Guide children to understand that the verb is not exact and does not give a clear picture of how the girl moved, how quickly she moved, and so on. Invite children to replace the verb *go* (or *goes*) with a more exact verb. Repeat children's suggestions after them and discuss with them just how those suggestions give a more exact picture.

Next, turn to page 72 of *At Home Around the World*. Tell children to imagine that they are writing a story about the people in the house at the bottom of the page. Have children join you on the floor in a story circle. Have them tell about the people in the house and what they are doing and saying. Have children refer to and use words from the chart as they tell the story. Begin the story by saying: **The woman whispers something. We struggle to hear it.**

To wrap up, ask: **Why was our story clear and interesting?** Guide children to see that the class tried to use exact verbs, which helped the story paint clear word pictures for the reader.

Independent Writing Practice   **Specific** *Do***s:** Write the general verb *do* on the board. Read the verb aloud and discuss its meaning. Then tell children to write an exact verb that could take its place. Have children write a sentence with their exact verb and illustrate the sentence, if they wish.

Reaching All Learners

BELOW LEVEL

To help children think of exact verbs, guide them in forming mental images. Say: **How do you put something on a table? Do you throw it? Do you drop it? Do you slide it? Do you toss it?**

ADVANCED

Have children write poems that include at least two exact verbs. Invite them to recite and act out their poems. Ask the class to tell how the exact verbs helped them paint pictures in their minds.

ENGLISH LANGUAGE LEARNERS

To illustrate each exact verb listed below *go*, display illustrations from books and magazines. Then act out each meaning as you say the verb. Have children echo.

© Harcourt

LESSON 4
Words to Describe Feelings

OBJECTIVES
- To understand the importance of words that describe feelings
- To identify words that describe feelings
- To write words that describe feelings

Oral Warm-Up   Invite children to join you in singing the first verse of "If You're Happy and You Know It." Explain that *happy* is a word that tells about a feeling. Ask them to use their smiles and movements to show that they are happy. When they have finished, tell children that you will all sing new words for this song, making faces and movements to match the words.

> **If you're tired and you know it, give a yawn.**
> **If you're silly and you know it, make a face.**
> **If you're sad and you know it, make a frown.**
> **If you're scared and you know it, cover your eyes.**
> **If you're mad and you know it, stomp your feet.**

Tell children that they have been singing about feelings and that, in this lesson, they will learn about words that help tell about feelings.

Teach/Model   Tell children that describing words help readers make pictures in their minds as they read. Explain that this is why writers often use describing words about feelings in their writing. Then create a Feelings Web. In the center oval, write the word *Feelings*. Then invite children to name a feeling. Write its name in a satellite oval and ask children to describe and act out that feeling. Encourage them to discuss that feeling, explaining what it is like, when it happens, and so on. Continue in the same way, having children suggest other familiar feelings.

HANDS ON ACTIVITY: FEELINGS MOBILES

Materials: hole-punched manila paper, hangers, and crayons or pencils

Directions:

1. Form small groups and have each group choose three feelings. Tell them to write each feeling at the top of a piece of hole-punched manila paper.

2. On other pieces of paper, have children draw a picture and write two words to tell about each feeling. Have groups attach their pictures to hangers with yarn. Then help them create a display of Feeling Mobiles.

© Harcourt

Guided Practice Remind children that writers often describe feelings. Explain that writers sometimes describe their own feelings and sometimes they describe the feelings of another person or a character in a story.

Choose one of the feelings from the Feeling Web. Write that term on the board and have children suggest words about that feeling. Discuss the words with them, talking about what the words mean, what they have to do with that feeling, and so on. Using the model below as a guide, work with children to build a list of "Words About _____."

<u>Words about Happy</u>

Glad	Grin
Smile	Clap
Cheer	Laugh

Independent Writing Practice **Feeling Parade:** Ask children to choose a feeling from the Feeling Web. Have children create a poster on which they put the name for that feeling. Then have them write three or four words that tell about it or go with it in some way. Encourage children to illustrate their posters. Then organize a Feeling Parade in which children display and explain their posters.

Extra Practice

Have children look through illustrated books and magazines. Ask them to point out pictures and illustrations that show people. Have children tell what they think each person is feeling. Add suggested feelings to the Feelings Web.

Reaching All Learners

BELOW LEVEL	ADVANCED	ENGLISH LANGUAGE LEARNERS
Discuss children's posters from the Independent Writing Practice. Encourage children to say their feeling words in sentences.	Invite children to expand the Independent Writing Practice by writing a story about someone who has the feeling they chose for Independent Writing Practice. Stories should be brief but should contain at least one example of someone having that particular feeling.	Point to each feeling word on the Feeling Web. Read it and have children echo. Share a common experience that might cause the feeling. To assess comprehension, invite children to talk about a time when they or someone they know had this feeling.

© Harcourt

LESSON 5
Words for Color, Size, and Shape

OBJECTIVES
- To identify and use describing words for color, size, and shape
- To write sentences with describing words

Oral Warm-Up Display attribute blocks or different sizes of colored-paper shapes. Ask children to choose a block or shape and tell its color, size, and shape. Use their responses to begin a Chart of Color, Size, and Shape Words.

Teach/Model Read the color, size, and shape words on the chart and tell children that these words are describing words. Remind children that good writers use describing words to help people make pictures in their minds. Explain that some describing words tell about color, size, and shape. Have children name the color, size, and shape words that are on the chart so far. Encourage children to suggest other words and to add those suggestions to the chart.

Reaching All Learners

BELOW LEVEL	**ADVANCED**	**ENGLISH LANGUAGE LEARNERS**
Divide children into small groups. Tell each group to find something large, something red, and something round. After three minutes, have groups identify the objects they found and compose an oral sentence describing each object.	Have children write a describing word in black, capital letters. Have them make a drawing that "dresses up" the describing word so that it looks like what it means.	Pair children with more proficient English speakers. Have one child write a single describing word—such as *large, red,* or *round*—on a sticky note. Then have that child's partner find an object in the room that matches that word. Have children exchange roles when they are done.

Guided Practice   Have children look at the picture on page 141 of *My Robot* and find the family pet, Prince. Ask children to imagine that Prince is missing and that they need to write a description that will help people find him. Have children share the pen as you work together to write the description. Prompt them to provide describing words that tell about color, size, and shape with questions such as the following: What color is Prince? How big is he? How would you describe his eyes? Are his ears big or small?

Periodically read aloud what you have written, pointing to each word. Praise individuals for their use of describing words and interesting ideas.

> Prince is a little, white dog.
> He has big ears.
> His eyes are small and round.

When children are satisfied with the description, have them read it aloud with you. Then have volunteers frame the words that tell about color (*white*), size (*little, big, small*), and shape (*round*). Add any new words to the Chart of Color, Size, and Shape Words.

Independent Writing Practice   **Describe a Toy:** Have each child draw a picture of a toy he or she really likes. Then have children write a sentence to describe that toy. If children have trouble thinking of words, suggest that they use words from the Chart of Color, Size, and Shape Words. When they are finished, have children share their sentences. Call attention to the describing words they use.

HANDS ON ACTIVITY: WHAT'S INSIDE?

Materials: box, and a classroom object

Directions:

1. Place an object (such as a teddy bear) in a box.
2. Divide the class into two groups. Have the first group look carefully at the object in the box. Then have that group dictate sentences that describe it. Write those sentences on the board.

3. When children have finished, read the sentences aloud, tracking them as you read. Ask children in the second group to guess what is inside the box. Open the box to reveal the answer.

LESSON 6
Words for Taste, Smell, Sound, and Feel

OBJECTIVES
- To identify and use describing words for taste, smell, sound, and feel
- To write sentences with describing words

Oral Warm-Up Ask children to think about what they like to eat for breakfast. Say: **I like to eat fruit and cereal for breakfast. The cereal I like best feels very crunchy in my mouth. And it makes crackly noises when I chew. It tastes and smells sweet because I like to put fruit on it.**

Have children take turns describing their own favorite breakfasts. As they talk, use their words to form a Chart of Taste, Smell, Sound, and Feel Words on the board.

Teach/Model Read aloud the words you have written on the chart, explaining that these words are describing words. Remind children that, in the previous lesson, they learned about describing words that tell about color, size, and shape. Tell children that, in this lesson, they will work with describing words that tell about taste, smell, sound, and feel. Then model thinking of taste, smell, sound, and feel words, adding the describing words to the chart as you model the process.

Model **I want to write about another of my favorite foods, muffins. Let's see. What do I know about how muffins feel? I remember the last time I touched a fresh muffin. It felt soft and warm. And I remember how it smelled while it was cooking in the oven. It smelled sweet. I couldn't wait to taste it! It tasted yummy.**

Sum up by writing the following sentences on the board: **The muffin feels warm in my hands. When I bite it, it tastes sweet and yummy. It is crunchy on the outside and soft inside.**

Read the sentences aloud, tracking with your finger as you read. Then ask children what each sentence tells you about the muffin. Then have them suggest other describing words they could use to tell about the muffin. Add their suggestions to the chart.

HANDS ON ACTIVITY: CAN YOU FEEL IT?

Materials: box with a cover, washcloth, apple, plush toy, small ball, paperclip, eraser, and other classroom items

Directions:
1. Without allowing children to see them, place all items into the box. Cover the box.
2. Have a child reach into the box, take an item, and, without looking at it, use sense words to tell about it.

Record the words in a Feelings List on the board.
3. When the child is ready, have the child guess what the item is. Have children repeat with additional items.

Guided Practice   Remind children that words about the senses can paint strong pictures in a reader's mind. Explain that the class will write about a boy named Lao. Tell children that Lao has gone to the beach with his family. Say: **Lao and his family are swimming. What do you think the water feels like? How does it taste and smell? What sound does it make when you jump and splash?**

Add children's responses to the chart. Then say: **Now Lao leaves the beach. At home, a kitten is playing in the yard. What does the kitten feel like? What sounds does it make? How does it smell?**

Again, add children's responses to the chart.

Then, using words from the chart, adapt something like the following: **We could just write:** *Lao went to the beach and went swimming. Then he went home and saw his kitten.* **Or we could write:** *Lao splashed in the cool, blue water. At home, he played with his tiny, white kitten. Its fur felt soft and fluffy. The kitten purred and meowed.* Ask: **Why is the second way to write the story so much better?** Guide children to understand that the second way uses sense words and paints a clear picture for the reader.

SHARING AND DISCUSSING

Display various items. Allow children to handle and examine each one. Ask how each tastes, smells, sounds, and feels. (Note that all questions will not be appropriate for all items.) Add any new describing words children mention to the chart of Taste, Smell, Sound, and Feel Words.

Independent Writing Practice   **Sense Words:** Write the name *Lao* on the board. Explain that Lao went to the beach and then played with his kitten. Now he is going to a birthday party. Have children write two sentences about what Lao does at the party. Tell children to use describing words to help readers see the party in their minds. Suggest children use words from the chart as well as new words of their own.

Reaching All Learners

BELOW LEVEL

Guide children in thinking of describing words. Explain that thinking about what birthday parties are like is a good way to figure out what is happening to Lao. Ask: **What do you hear at a birthday party? What do you see and taste?**

ADVANCED

Have children challenge one another with riddles. Explain that each riddle should include questions about at least two of the senses. Provide the model: **I am flat and smooth and I make no noise. But I make a crinkly sound if you crumple me into a ball. What am I?** (a piece of paper)

ENGLISH LANGUAGE LEARNERS

Work closely with children to be certain they understand describing words. Provide items such as a banana, a soft plush toy, and a hand-held bell as you reinforce vocabulary.

© Harcourt

LESSON 7
Words for How Many

OBJECTIVES
- To identify number words in sentences
- To write number words in sentences

Oral Warm-Up Invite children to join you in reciting "Five Little Monkeys Jumping on the Bed."

> Five Little Monkeys jumping on the bed!
> One fell off and bumped his head.
> Mama called the doctor, and the doctor said,
> "No more monkeys jumping on the bed."

Ask: **How many monkeys were jumping on the bed at the beginning of the rhyme?** (five) Next, ask: **How many monkeys fell off?** (one) Explain that the numbers *five* and *one* tell how many. Write the words *five* and *one* on the board. Then have volunteers come to the board and write the numeral that corresponds to each number word.

Teach/Model Explain that writers use describing words to tell how many. Point out that writers usually do not write numbers in sentences. Instead, they use the words that name the numbers. Direct children's attention to page 188 of *Little Bear's Friend*. Ask: **How many bears do you see in the tree?** After children answer, write the word *one* as you begin a How Many List on the board. Then write this sentence: *I see one bear.* Track the words with your finger as you read the sentence aloud.

Next, have children turn to page 193 of *Little Bear's Friend*. Ask: **How many squirrels are in the tree?** Add the word *two* to the list. Then write: *I see two squirrels.* Again, track the words as you read them. Continue by asking how many people are on page 202. Add the word *three* to the list. Then follow the same procedure as you write: *I see three people.* Finally, turn to page 194. Ask: **How many birds do you see?** Add the word *four* to the list. Then write this sentence, tracking the words as you read them aloud: *I see four birds.*

Continue by adding the words *five, six, seven, eight, nine,* and *ten* to the list. Work with children to make up a sentence for each of these number words. Write the sentences on the board, tracking the words as you read them aloud. Sum up by saying that there is a spelled-out number word for each number that we can use.

HANDS ON ACTIVITY: NUMBER CONCENTRATION

Materials: index cards and markers

Directions:

1. Write numerals *1* through *5* and the number words *one* through *five* on separate index cards.
2. Have children scramble the cards and lay them out facedown. Have the first player flip a card and put it aside. Then have the child flip other cards until he or she finds a numeral or number-word card that matches the first one. Each time a match is made, the player turns the remaining cards facedown and lets another child have a turn.
3. After everyone has had a turn, start a new game with cards numbered *six*/6 through *ten*/10.

© Harcourt

Guided Practice   Write the following sentence frame on the board:

> I see _____ fingers.

Remind children that writers use number words in sentences to describe how many. Display the How Many List. Hold up one finger. Ask children how many fingers they see. Then invite a volunteer to come to the board and write the word *one* in the sentence. Read the finished sentence aloud, having the children echo. Then hold up two fingers and ask a volunteer to come the board, erase the old number, and write the new word that tells how many. Continue in the same way through *10/ten*.

Independent Writing Practice   **Animal Sentences:** Have children write two sentences about animals. Tell them to include a different number word in each sentence. Encourage them to draw a picture for each sentence to show how many animals it describes.

★ **Extra Practice**

Have pairs write number words one through *ten*—one number on each of ten index cards. Have one partner hold number words *one* through *five* and the other hold *six* through *ten*. Take children on a classroom walk. Point out posters, book covers, and other items in the classroom. For each, ask: **How many ___ do you see?** Have children hold up the correct number card.

Reaching All Learners

BELOW LEVEL

Provide paperclips. Have children count out piles of paperclips from one to ten and lay all ten groups of paperclips on a table. Tell children to write number words from *one* to *ten*—one word on each of ten sticky notes. Then have children stick each note below the correct group.

ADVANCED

Challenge children to copy the number list and then extend it to *fifteen*. Have them write sentences for *eleven* through *fifteen*.

ENGLISH LANGUAGE LEARNERS

To aid children in understanding numerals and their corresponding number words, display a card—with the numeral and the number word—for *1/one* through *10/ten*. Arrange items of a corresponding amount for all ten numbers. Point to each item as you count it. Then point to the numeral and the number word.

© Harcourt

LESSON 8
Capitalization

OBJECTIVES
- To capitalize days of the week and months of the year
- To capitalize names of cities, states, and streets
- To capitalize people's titles

Oral Warm-Up On the board, write several pairs of capital and small letters, including *Aa, Cc, Ii, Mm, Pp, Rr, Ss,* and *Tt.* Point out the capital and small letter in each pair. Then tell children that you are going to give them some sentences and that it will be up to some volunteers to point out the capital letters in those sentences.

Then write the following sentence on the board, tracking the words as you read: *I saw him on Main Street.* Call for a volunteer and guide him or her to correctly identify the capital *I, M,* and *S.* Continue in the same way with these sentences:

> *Paul visited Texas.*
> *Tina was born in June.*
> *I ate popcorn at Aaron's house.*

Teach/Model Remind children that capital letters are used only for certain words and that they help readers understand what kinds of words writers are using. On the board, write the following rules for capitalizing words, saving the list for use later in the lesson.

Use a Capital Letter
- to begin a sentence
- to write the word *I*
- to begin a person's name
- to begin the name of a day or month
- to begin the name of a street, city, or state

On the board, write the names of several days of the week, underlining each capital letter. Repeat with months of the year as well as the street, city, and state address of your school. Finally, write the following on the board: *Mr. Salas, Ms. Lee, Dr. Wong, Aunt Mia, Uncle Bob.* Explain that words like *Mr., Dr.,* and *Uncle* are titles and that titles tell more about a person. Point out that titles get capitalized. Add the words *to begin someone's title* to the list on the board and have a volunteer underline the capital letter in each title from the Oral Warm-Up.

HANDS ON ACTIVITY: FIND THE CAPITALS

Materials: magazines and books

Directions:
1. Form groups and review the capitalization rules on the board.
2. Have groups search magazines and books for an example of each rule.
3. When the groups have found all examples, have them form a circle and share their findings.

© Harcourt

Guided Practice   Provide a baseball cap or other kind of cap, reminding children that this is the Capitalization Cap. Tell children that the cap will help them show when capital letters are being used correctly. Then review the capitalization rules developed earlier, keeping them visible for children.

Write the following sentences on the board. Read each aloud, tracking the words as you read. Then give a volunteer the Capitalization Cap and ask him or her to fix any mistakes with capital letters in the first sentence and to wave the cap in the air for each correction. (The day of the week, *Monday,* needs to begin with a capital letter.)

> We go to school on monday.
> did you see dr. Long?
> Fara and i like the month of may.
> My aunt Jan lives in ohio.
> The store is on king street.
> Can i speak to' mr. Park this afternoon?

(Monday, Did, Dr.; I, May; Aunt, Ohio; King; Street; I, Mr.)

Independent Writing Practice   **Sentences About a Trip:** Tell children to write three sentences about a make-believe trip. In their sentences, have children name the month for the trip, the city or state to which they will travel, and the names of the people who will go with them. Invite children to illustrate their sentences.

★ **Extra Practice**

Form small groups and have each group write an example word that goes with each capitalization rule. Have groups compare their words when they finish.

Reaching All Learners

BELOW LEVEL	**ADVANCED**	**ENGLISH LANGUAGE LEARNERS**
Take children on a classroom walk, pointing out examples of capitalization rules, such as months and days on a classroom calendar, the capital letters in names, etc. Have children write the capital letter that begins each word.	Challenge children to research a place they have always wanted to visit. Have them create a poster about this place. Remind them to make sure they correctly capitalize the place names on the poster.	The days of the week are not capitalized in all languages. To emphasize English capitalization rules, display a calendar page. Read aloud the names of the days, having children echo. Highlight the capital letter in each day.

© Harcourt

LESSON 1
Sentence Starters

OBJECTIVES

- To identify the first words of sentences in speech and in print
- To explore how writers begin sentences in different ways
- To vary sentence beginnings
- To write on a topic of choice

Oral Warm-Up Tell children that they will be playing a listening game. Say: **I'm going to say a sentence. Listen for the first word I say.** Then say: **It looks like it could rain this afternoon.** Ask children to identify the first word you said (*it*). Continue with other sentences that begin with different words. Invite children to supply their own sentences and call on volunteers to identify the first word of these, as well.

Teach/Model Point out that the sentences in the Oral Warm-Up began with a variety of words. Explain that good writers make sure their sentences do not all begin the same way. On the board, write:

> The bird was born. The bird lived in a tree. The bird grew fast.

Help children to read the sentences aloud. Draw circles around the first word of each sentence (*the, the, the*) and elicit that all the sentences begin the same way. Then display *The Story of a Blue Bird*. Say:

> **This story begins sort of like the one I wrote on the board, but you'll find that this book is more interesting than my story! One reason is that the writer of this book used different words to begin his sentences.**

Have children listen for the opening words of sentences as you read pages 13–16 aloud. Then reread the sentences slowly, and have children name the opening word of each sentence. Write the first few words of each sentence on the board and draw a circle around the first word. Compare the circled words. Point out that almost every sentence has a different beginning. Sum up by saying: **It's fun to read a book when the sentences begin in different and interesting ways.**

HANDS ON ACTIVITY: QUESTION OPENERS

Materials: cards with the words *why, when, where, what,* and *who*

Directions:

1. Place one of each word card on each table.
2. Have children write questions that begin with each of the five words and end with a question mark.
3. Have children share their sentences with each other.

© Harcourt

Guided Practice   Remind children that stories are most interesting when writers start their sentences in different ways. Ask children to suggest topics for a group story. Have children choose from among these topics. Write a title at the top of a piece of chart paper.

Then have a volunteer suggest an opening sentence for the story. Copy the sentence as it is told to you. Have another volunteer identify the first word of the sentence and circle it. Call for another volunteer to continue the story, beginning the next sentence with a different word. Circle the first word of this sentence, as well.

Continue for about 8–10 sentences, asking children to read the list of circled (opening) words from time to time. Read the finished product aloud. Stress that each sentence of the story begins differently. Say: **When sentences all start in different ways, the story can be lots of fun to read.**

Independent Writing Practice   Circling First Words: Have children write 4–5 sentences on a topic of interest to them. Ask children to circle the first word of each sentence as a reminder to begin each sentence with a different word. Children should illustrate their writing and read it aloud to a partner, emphasizing the different beginning to each sentence.

SHARING AND DISCUSSING

Have children look at samples of their written work from earlier in the year. Ask them to go through their writing and make a list of the first words used in each sentence. Have children talk to partners about whether they used lots of different words or only a few.

Reaching All Learners

BELOW LEVEL

Have children write one sentence per line during the Independent Writing Practice. This will help them organize their papers and see more clearly where the sentences begin and end. Remind children to end each sentence with a period.

ADVANCED

Have children make a tally chart showing all the words used to begin the sentences in *The Story of a Blue Bird*. Ask them to find the number of different words used to begin sentences and the word used to begin the greatest number of sentences, as well.

ENGLISH LANGUAGE LEARNERS

Children new to the English language may not be certain how to divide ideas into sentences. Read children's work aloud, pausing and lowering your voice at the end of a sentence. Help children put periods where they belong.

LESSON 2
More Sentence Starters

OBJECTIVES

- To identify the beginnings of sentences
- To explore how writers begin sentences in different ways
- To make a list of "good sentence starters"
- To write on a topic of choice

Oral Warm-Up   Explain that you will say either one word or a group of words. Ask volunteers to determine which you said. Say the following words and phrases: **pizza** (word), **on the school bus** (group of words), **my little brother** (group of words), **I** (word), **dimes and pennies** (group of words), **the** (word), and **the baseball game** (group of words). Continue with other examples as desired. Mention that all of these could be sentence starters, and that good writers often begin their sentences in different ways.

Teach/Model   Write these two sentences on the board:

> Wham! went the big red ball against the fence
> The big red ball hit the fence.

Have children read the sentences and identify the opening word or group of words in each (possible answers: *Wham!; The big red ball*). Draw out or explain that the word *Wham!* is more lively and dramatic than the phrase *the big red ball*. Emphasize that there is nothing wrong with a sentence that begins *The big red ball,* but stress that *Wham!* is a more interesting sentence starter.

Display *Frog and Toad All Year.* Tell children that you are going to make a list of some good ways that the writer of this book began sentences. Open the book and page through it, looking for good sentence beginnings. Model this process as follows:

> **Model**   I like the sentence on page 42 that begins with the word *if.* Arnold Lobel wrote *If you stand near the stove,* but you could write other sentences beginning with *if,* such as *If I were a pirate* or *If I could run like a lion. . .* Another sentence starter I like is *When I was. . .* I can think of all kinds of interesting sentences that begin that way!

Continue with *Soon, What. . .,* and *Did you. . . ?* Write these sentence openers on chart paper and title the list Good Sentence Starters.

HANDS ON ACTIVITY: DIFFERENT STARTERS

Materials: pictures of animals

Directions:

1. Place a picture of an animal on each table.
2. Have children write a sentence about the animal. Tell them that each child at a given table must begin their sentences in different ways.

© Harcourt

Guided Practice Give a trade picture book or chapter book to each pair of children. Ask children to read through their book together and note words and phrases that are used to open sentences. Have them work together to choose 1–2 opening words or phrases from the book that they think are especially good sentence starters. Ask them to copy each choice onto a sticky note and place the note on the board.

Next, have children share the sentence starters they found with the whole group. Ask children to explain what they liked about the word or phrase and why they thought it was a good sentence starter. Add these ideas to your chart of "good sentence starters."

Independent Writing Practice **Using Good Sentence Starters:** Have children write 3 or 4 sentences on a topic of their choice. Instruct children to begin at least one sentence with a word or phrase from the "good sentence starters" chart and encourage them to be creative in beginning other sentences. Have children read their work to a partner and point out the sentence beginnings. Allow time for illustrations as well.

SHARING AND DISCUSSING

Write the following sentences on the board: *I went outside. I went to the store. I went to the park. I went back home.* Have children read the sentences aloud. Point out that the sentences all begin the same way. Have children help you revise the sentences so they begin differently.

Reaching All Learners

BELOW LEVEL

For the Guided Practice, assign below level learners a partner who is a more fluent reader. Have the partner read sentences aloud; then have both partners discuss each sentence beginning and choose the ones they like best.

ADVANCED

Have children work in pairs. Have them make their own lists of "good sentence starters," which may include models that they have seen elsewhere (such as those discussed in the lesson) and words and phrases of their own.

ENGLISH LANGUAGE LEARNERS

Work with English language learners in a small group during the Guided Practice. Read sentences aloud one by one as children look on. Use pantomime and real objects to provide vocabulary help as needed.

© Harcourt

LESSON 3
Short Sentences and Long Sentences

OBJECTIVES

- To listen for different sentence lengths
- To explore how writers vary sentence lengths
- To write sentences of different lengths
- To write about a favorite animal

Oral Warm-Up Display *Fishing Bears*. Tell children that you will read some of the sentences in the book. Ask them whether the sentences you read are short, long, or in between. Read aloud the second sentence on page 74 (long), the second sentence on page 75 (short), and the second sentence on page 78 (in between). Continue with other sentences from the book.

Teach/Model Explain that good writers use short sentences, long sentences, and in-between-sized sentences to make their writing more interesting to read. Point out that some sentences in *Fishing Bears* have only four or five words, while others have more than ten.

Tell children that you are going to write a few sentences about ducks. Explain that you want to vary the lengths of your sentences. Model this process as follows, writing the italicized words on the board as you say them:

> **I'll start by saying** *Ducks are birds that live near the water.* **That sentence isn't very long or very short; it's in between. I'll try for a different length for my next sentence. Let's try this:** *Baby ducks hatch from eggs.* **That sentence is pretty short. Now would be a good time for a long one:** *When they get a little older, the babies will learn how to fly and how to swim.* **I'll end my work with two more sentences:** *Can you quack like a baby duck? I can!*

Have children read the sentences aloud. Review which sentences are long, short, and in between. Emphasize that the writing sounds better because the sentence lengths change.

HANDS ON ACTIVITY: HOW MANY WORDS?

Materials: none

Directions:

1. Write the numbers *3*, *5*, and *7* on the board.
2. Have children work with a partner to write three sentences on any topics they like. One sentence must include three words, one five words, and one seven words. Remind children to be sure that their sentences make sense.

© Harcourt

Guided Practice   Reread *Fishing Bears,* calling children's attention to the lengths of sentences. Choose an animal your class has studied. At the top of a sheet of chart paper, write:

WHAT WE KNOW ABOUT _____

Then tell children that you will all work together to write sentences about this animal. Add that their work must include sentences that are short, sentences that are long, and sentences that are in between.

Call on volunteers to contribute sentences. Write each on the chart paper. Ask children to determine whether each sentence is short, long, or in between. If children suggest sentences that are all roughly the same lengths, guide them to make changes by saying: **That's a great idea; let's see if we can make your sentence a little longer** or **Who would like to suggest a short sentence now?** Collect about 7–8 sentences. Then have volunteers read each sentence in turn. Point out the changing sentence lengths.

Independent Writing Practice   **Animal Writing:** Have children select an animal other than the one you chose for the Guided Practice. Have them write 3–5 sentences telling what they know about their animal. Ask them to vary the lengths of their sentences so that they have at least one short sentence, at least one long sentence, and at least one that is in between. Have children illustrate their work and give their writing titles.

> **SHARING AND DISCUSSING**
>
> Have pairs of children read through classroom books. Ask them to find examples of sentences that are long, short, and in between. Have them talk about what they discovered.

Reaching All Learners

BELOW LEVEL	ADVANCED	ENGLISH LANGUAGE LEARNERS
If children have difficulty telling whether their ideas form a full sentence, have them ask themselves: *Do these words tell a complete idea? Does it put a picture in my head?*	For the Independent Writing Practice, have children write their sentences on sentence strips so they can be arranged in different orders. Have children decide which arrangement of sentences sounds best and makes the most sense.	Offer children extra practice in recognizing and constructing complete sentences. Write *I can ride my bike, Sam is my friend,* and *It is lunchtime* on sentence strips. Cut each sentence in two parts. Have children reassemble the sentences so they make sense.

© Harcourt

LESSON 4
More Short and Long Sentences

OBJECTIVES

- To classify sentences according to their lengths
- To explore how to increase sentence lengths
- To lengthen existing sentences

Oral Warm-Up Ask children to create oral sentences that are on any topic and that are short, long, or in between. Have volunteers say their sentences aloud. Ask classmates to classify each sentence according to its length.

Teach/Model Remind children that writing is more interesting to read when sentences are of different lengths. Say: **Sometimes people write lots of sentences that are very short. Here's an example.** Display four index cards on which you have written the words *a, have, rabbit,* and *I*. Give each card to a volunteer. Challenge these four children to come to the front of the room and form a row so that their cards form a complete sentence. (I have a rabbit.) Encourage children to carry out this task without talking.

Establish that this is a short sentence, one that contains only four words. Then say: **I'd like to change the length of this sentence and make it a little longer.** Model how to increase the length of this sentence:

> **Model** I'll write the word *furry* on this card. I wonder where the word *furry* could go in the sentence? That's right, before *rabbit*. Carlo, would you hold the card right there, please? Let's read the new sentence—*I have a furry rabbit*. Let me add some more words at the beginning. This card says *sister*. This one says *and*. This one says *My*. Who can tell where these cards should go?. . .

Have children use the cards to form the new sentence *My sister and I have a furry rabbit*. Ask children to read the sentence one word at a time. Point out that by adding words, you can change the length of the sentence.

HANDS ON ACTIVITY: ANIMAL TRACK POSTERS

Materials: butcher paper and markers or paints

Directions:

1. Divide children into small groups. Have children draw or paint animal tracks on butcher paper.

2. Ask each child to write a short sentence and a long sentence to tell about the tracks on their poster.

Guided Practice Make and display index cards with the following words: *soup, Tom, likes.* As before, ask children to order these cards so they make a complete sentence (*Tom likes soup*). Establish that this sentence is very short. Ask volunteers for single words and short phrases that could make the sentence longer. For each suggestion, write each new word or words on a card, give each card to a volunteer, and challenge children to line up so their cards say the new sentence. Have the class read the new sentence aloud.

Then collect the new cards, give the original three cards (*Tom, likes, soup*) to three other children, and continue with other suggestions. Possible changes include *Tom likes chicken soup, Tom likes to eat hot soup,* and *Tom likes soup when it's cold outside.* Remind children that these sentences are longer and can help children produce more lively and interesting writing.

Independent Writing Practice **Make It Longer:** On the board, write the sentence:

> I have a hat.

Have children read it aloud. Instruct children to add words of their own to your sentence so it is longer. Possibilities might include *I have a red firefighter's hat, I have a hat and a pair of mittens,* and *I have a hat that makes me look like a duck.* Have children write their new sentence on a sheet of paper, read it aloud to a partner, and draw a picture to go with it.

SHARING AND DISCUSSING

Have children read through *How to Be a Nature Detective* on pages 101–115. Ask them to look for the shortest and the longest sentences in the story. Have them mark the longest sentence with a red sticky and the shortest with a blue sticky. Have them compare their answers with other children's.

Reaching All Learners

BELOW LEVEL	ADVANCED	ENGLISH LANGUAGE LEARNERS
For the Independent Writing Practice, have children write each word on an index card. Then have children place the cards in the proper order on their paper and glue them in place to form their sentence. This will help children keep track of which words they have used.	Have children work with a partner. Ask each child to write a sentence of 3–4 words. Have children exchange sentences. Instruct children to write a new and longer sentence based on their partner's original. Have children share their work with others.	Have children begin by adding just one word to a sentence, such as changing *We can run* to *We can run fast* or changing *My dog barked* to *My black dog barked.* Give children a card with the new word on it and help them place it correctly in the sentence.

© Harcourt

LESSON 5
Rhythm and Sound

OBJECTIVES
- To listen and respond to a poem
- To listen for the way writing sounds
- To identify sentences that sound good
- To write on a topic of interest

Oral Warm-Up Tell children that you will read a poem aloud. Explain that you would like them to pay close attention to the way the poem sounds. Then read aloud the poem "To Walk in Warm Rain," on page 149E of *Trophies TE,* or substitute another short rhythmic poem of your choice. Lead a discussion about the poem and the way it sounds. Elicit or explain that the poem has rhythm and rhyme. Emphasize the repetition of words and sounds (such as *dr–* in *drip like a drain*). Wrap up by saying: **Good writing can be lots of fun to read aloud. I like the ideas in this poem, and I also like the way the poem sounds.**

Teach/Model Explain that writers often read their work aloud when they are done just to see how it sounds. Point out that if writing does not sound right, writers make changes. Display *The Puddle* on pages 127–146. Say: **This book is not a poem, but I think you'll agree that many of the sentences in this book sound exactly right.** Then model how to listen for the way sentences sound. Read through the book, pausing to comment on the pages as follows:

Model On page 130, the writer wrote: *. . .and went to sail my boat in the largest puddle I could find.* This part of the sentence has a rhythm that I really like, even though it is not poetry. He could have written: *. . .and went to sail my boat in a big puddle,* but I'm glad he didn't. This way has more rhythm. I also like this line on page 131: *"Nice boat," he said.* That line is short and snappy and funny. I can almost hear a real frog saying it!

Continue through the book, pointing out sentences that sound good.

LITERATURE ACTIVITY: POEMS

Materials: books of poetry

Directions:
1. Have children choose a poem from books of poetry available in the classroom.
2. Have children practice reading aloud either the entire poem or a section they especially like.
3. Have children read their poems aloud to others.

© Harcourt

Guided Practice Explain that children can use the process you modeled to check the sound of their own writing. Ask children to suppose that more animals came along to play in the puddle that is described in the book. Say: **What would these animals do? What would they say?** Accept a suggestion from a volunteer and write it on the board. Then say: **Let's read this again so we can really listen to how this sentence sounds.** Read it two or three times and ask for volunteers to read it, too. Say: **It can be helpful to have someone else read your work.**

Then ask the child who proposed the sentence if it sounds right. Ask guiding questions such as: **Does this sentence have rhythm? Are the words where you want them to be?** Emphasize that the sentence must sound right to the person who wrote it. Make changes if necessary. Then repeat with suggestions from other children.

Independent Writing Practice **Read It Aloud:** Have children write on a topic of interest. Instruct them to write at least three sentences. Then have them read their work aloud while listening carefully to the way it sounds. Ask them to exchange papers with a partner and have partners read each other's work aloud, as well. Encourage children to make changes as needed to make the sentence sound better. When they are satisfied, have them draw a picture.

SHARING AND DISCUSSING

Ask children to take turns reading *The Puddle* aloud with a partner. Have partners identify the sentence in the book that sounds best or is most fun to read aloud. Ask them to share this sentence with the rest of the class and to explain why they like it.

Reaching All Learners

BELOW LEVEL	ADVANCED	ENGLISH LANGUAGE LEARNERS
To help children learn to listen to their own writing, have them read simple texts aloud as much as possible. Encourage them to read with expression and to repeat each sentence or page until they can listen to their voice, rather than focusing so much on the words.	Have children experiment with using different voices to read their sentences aloud. Ask them what their words would sound like if they were spoken by a turtle/a teacher/a small child/a teenager. Ask them to share their ideas with a partner.	When possible, offer English language learners two possible sentences and ask them to choose the one that sounds best. For instance, ask children whether they prefer *I have a sandwich for lunch* or *My lunch is a sandwich.*

© Harcourt

LESSON 6
More Rhythm and Sound

OBJECTIVES
- To listen for repetition
- To listen for the way writing sounds
- To identify sentences and groups of sentences that sound right
- To write sentences that sound good

Oral Warm-Up Tell children that you will read a part of the book *Poppleton Everyday* aloud. Ask them to listen for the way the writer uses words. Then read aloud pages 164–167. As you read, emphasize the repetition of *It was vast! It was enormous!* and the sentences beginning *He lay. . .* Then ask children to talk about what they noticed. Elicit that there was a lot of repetition in the selection. Sum up by saying: **As you know, writers like to begin sentences in different ways. But sometimes, using repetition—even at the beginning of sentences—can make writing sound special.**

Teach/Model Tell children that it can be important to read not just one sentence aloud, but several at a time. Explain that, just as in *Poppleton Everyday*, sentences sometimes go together in ways that make them all sound good. Say: **I'm going to write three sentences that begin the same way. I'm going to pay attention to how they each sound, and I'm going to think about how they sound together.** Model this process as follows, writing sentences on the board as you speak:

Model I'm going to start my sentences with *If I were a bluebird.* I'll write that here. Let's see. *If I were a bluebird, I would sing in the morning. If I were a bluebird, I would fly in the afternoon.* I like the way those sentences sound together. They have a nice rhythm. *If I were a bluebird, then at night I would try to go to sleep.* No. That doesn't sound quite right. It's too long, and the words don't come in the right order. I think I'll try *If I were a bluebird, I would sleep at night.*

Read the completed work aloud, emphasizing the rhythm and repetition. Have children repeat.

HANDS ON ACTIVITY: MY LUNCH

Materials: none

Directions:

1. Have children choose one describing word to complete the sentence *My lunch is. . .* (*gooey, crunchy, tasty*).
2. Have children write this sentence on a sentence strip.
3. Have children work with a small group. Ask them to put their sentences in order so the result sounds good.
4. Have them read their work aloud to others.

Guided Practice Tell children that they will be writing as a group. Say: **This writing will be several sentences long. Each sentence will begin the same way:** *When I grow up. . .* Write this sentence starter on the board and have volunteers finish it. Copy their work onto the board and read it aloud. After every two or three suggestions, have children read the entire work thus far. Ask whether the work as a whole sounds good: whether sentences are in the right order, whether children can hear rhythm in the words, and if children would like to suggest changes. Make changes as needed, but emphasize simply listening to the words. From time to time, make comments such as: **I like the way Marsha's sentence** *When I grow up I will be old* **sounds next to Tobias's sentence** *When I grow up I will be tall.*

Independent Writing Practice **When I Was Little:** Have children write 3–5 sentences that begin with the phrase *When I was little. . .* Instruct them to read their work aloud to themselves and then to a partner. Remind them to listen to the way the words sound and the way the sentences fit together. Have children illustrate their work. Use the pages to create a class book entitled *When We Were Little.*

> ⭐ **Extra Practice**
>
> Have children work in small groups. Have one child say a sentence that begins with the word *Someday,* as in *Someday I will learn to ride a horse.* Continue with each successive child repeating the previous sentence and adding a new one.

Reaching All Learners

BELOW LEVEL

If children struggle with the mechanics of writing, they may have difficulty paying attention to the sounds of their sentences. Consider asking classmates to serve as a scribe for these children. Ask the scribe to take dictation from the other child so the writer is free to focus on the sound of his or her sentences.

ADVANCED

Have children write other pieces that involve the repetition described in this lesson. Possible starters include *I dreamed. . ., If I could fly. . .,* and *When summer comes.* Alternatively, have children choose their own beginnings.

ENGLISH LANGUAGE LEARNERS

Many English language learners children are not yet accustomed to the rhythms of the English language. Help these children by pairing them with a native English speaker. Ask the native speaker to listen to the English language learner's sentences and make suggestions of his or her own.

LESSON 7
More About Sentences

OBJECTIVES
- To share knowledge and information
- To brainstorm ideas
- To take notes on a science or social studies topic
- To turn notes into fluent sentences

Oral Warm-Up Choose a familiar animal such as a cow. Go around as quickly as possible, asking children to say something they know about cows. Encourage children to keep their comments very brief. Make notes on the board (such as *milk* to summarize the comment *Cows give milk*). Mention that these notes are helpful reminders of what people said. Wrap up by reading through the notes with children.

Teach/Model Explain that the Oral Warm-Up activity is sometimes called *brainstorming*. Say: **When you brainstorm, you get lots of ideas all at once, like the rain and the lightning in a real thunderstorm.** Explain that it would take too much time for people to write full sentences for all the ideas they have while brainstorming. Tell children that people usually make notes and write full sentences later, just as you did on the board.

Explain that you are going to turn children's notes on cows into full sentences. Say: **I have to think about how my sentences sound. I need to be sure to vary the lengths of my sentences, too.** Then model this process as follows:

Model Sandi said that cows were farm animals, and Paris mentioned that they give milk. I could say *Cows are farm animals. They give milk.* But I'm going to put those two ideas into one sentence instead: *Cows are farm animals that give milk.* Now, I want a longer sentence. I'll use Ryan's idea that cows eat grass, and I'll say: *If you go to a farm, you will probably see cows eating grass. . .*

Continue for 3–4 sentences. Read aloud the entire piece of writing and point out how the sentences sound together.

HANDS ON ACTIVITY: COMIC STRIPS

Materials: comic strips cut from daily newspapers, with the words removed

Directions:

1. Give each child a comic strip. Point out that the words have been removed.

2. Ask children to write a story that tells what might be going on in this comic strip.

3. Have children share their work with a partner.

Guided Practice Have children tell what they know about another animal, such as a horse. Follow the procedure outlined in the Teach/Model activity to generate a list of notes about horses. Read the list with children. Then invite them to express one or more of these ideas in a single sentence. Remind children that their sentences should be varied, interesting, and informative, and that they also should sound good. Write children's suggestions on the board. Read old and new sentences aloud to check that they work well together.

Independent Writing Practice **Brainstorming:** Have children form small groups. Ask them to work in their groups to brainstorm everything they know about trees, birds, or a science or social studies topic your class has studied. Assign a scribe in each group to make notes on chart paper. Then hang the chart paper so it is visible to everyone in the group. Have children create sentences based on the notes their groups put together. Remind children to check to make sure their writing sounds good and that their sentences are varied and fit together. Leave time for illustrations as well.

> ⭐ **Extra Practice**
>
> Have children brainstorm about sleep. Explain that the writer of *Sleep Is for Everyone* took the information he had about sleep and turned it into sentences to write the book. Read the book aloud. Invite children to discuss how the writer turned the book into sentences.

Reaching All Learners

BELOW LEVEL	ADVANCED	ENGLISH LANGUAGE LEARNERS
Copying from a chart is difficult for some children. For the Independent Writing Practice, you may want to copy group notes onto index cards for these children. In this way, the notes will be easier to see and manipulate.	During the Guided Practice, ask advanced learners to make the notes on the board when children offer information. Remind them to use large handwriting so their words will show up from a distance.	As you make notes on the board during these activities, add simple sketches to help English language learners associate words with objects. Encourage note takers in the Independent Writing Practice to do the same.

© Harcourt

LESSON 8
Editing

OBJECTIVES
- To explore the editing process
- To identify and fix errors of capitalization, punctuation, spelling, and sentence structure
- To write on a topic of choice

Oral Warm-Up Tell children that they will be playing a listening game. Say: *Where is the eraser?* Ask children to determine from your intonation whether your sentence should end with a period, a question mark, or an exclamation mark (question mark). Ask children to explain how they know. Continue with other examples such as *This is a chair* and *We're the winners!*

Teach/Model Display the book *Baboon* on page 221 and tell children that you will write the first part of the book on the board. Read aloud the first two lines of the book, using ordinary expression, as you write *baboon opened him sleepy eyes ahead wuz great forest?* Ask children if you have written this sentence perfectly. Elicit or explain that you have not.

Explain that good writers use the editing process when they finish a piece of writing. Point out that writers often make mistakes when they put together a first draft, and that the editing includes finding and fixing those mistakes. Explain that editing involves checking spelling, punctuation, and capitalization, along with making sure the words are in the right places and that the ideas make sense. Then model the editing process. Say:

> **Model** There's a problem in the first word. The word *baboon* is a name in this book. It also starts a sentence. For both reasons, the first *b* should be a capital letter. I'll fix that. What else? I wrote *him*, but I needed a different word. Listen: *Baboon opened his sleepy eyes*. . .That's right, the real word is *his*, not *him*. I need to change *m* to *s* so I have the proper word.

Continue through the piece with children's input, fixing the spelling of *was*, inserting the missing word *the*, and changing the final question mark to a period. Read the edited work aloud. Point out that the sentences make sense. Add that it is much easier to read the edited sentences.

Reaching All Learners

BELOW LEVEL	ADVANCED	ENGLISH LANGUAGE LEARNERS
Offer children alternatives for the Teach/Model activity. Ask: *Should the first word be* baboon *with a lower-case* b, *or should it be* baboon *with a capital* B? Many children find it easier to pick the correct choice from two alternatives.	Have children write three sentences. Instruct them to write one sentence that ends with a period, one that ends with a question mark, and one that ends with an exclamation mark. Have them edit their work and trade papers with a partner for further editing.	Have children focus on each area of the editing process sequentially. First, ask them to think about punctuation marks. Then have them look for issues with capitalization. Finally, have them investigate spelling errors and missing words.

© Harcourt

Guided Practice   Write the following words on the board:

> this book is abowt a baboon teh baboon Wants find
> out about? the world he Asks! his mother to help him?

Explain that this piece of writing tells about the book *Baboon*. Point out that this description contains some errors that need to be fixed. Remind children that they can find and fix these errors by using the editing process.

Go around the room, asking volunteers to point out mistakes and explain how to correct them. Review each suggestion by saying: **Yes, the word *about* is not spelled correctly** or **You're right, I need to put a period after the word *world*.** Ask guiding questions if needed, such as **Are capital letters in the right places?** or **What punctuation marks do we need?** Help children read the words aloud and determine punctuation from the intonation they use as they speak. Read the piece aloud when it is fixed. (*This book is about a baboon. The baboon wants to find out about the world. He asks his mother to help him.*) Ask children if the writing makes sense and is easy to read. Emphasize that these are the goals of editing.

Independent Writing Practice   **Editing:** Have children write on a subject of their choice. Remind them to edit their work after they have written a draft. Check children's papers as they work and give them plenty of feedback. Say, for instance: **Read this sentence again, and see if all the words are in the right order** or **Yes, I'm glad you changed that period to a question mark—that sentence really is a question.** Ask children to trade papers with a classmate and edit each other's work. Allow time for illustrations.

> ⭐ **Extra Practice**
>
> On a sheet of paper, recopy the first three lines of page 236 in *Baboon*. Omit punctuation marks, however, and use only lower case letters. Have children work in pairs and give each pair a copy of this sheet. Ask them to fill in the missing punctuation marks and change letters to capitals as necessary.

HANDS ON ACTIVITY: WRITE DIRECTIONS

Materials: none

Directions:

1. Have children explain in writing how to sharpen a pencil, climb a pole, or carry out some other activity.

2. Have children trade papers with a partner. Ask partners to help each other edit for punctuation, capitalization, spelling, and content.

Approaches to Writing Instruction

A variety of approaches to writing instruction may happen in the classroom at any given time. Emergent and early writers will benefit from the language experience approach, shared writing, and interactive writing. Each of these approaches may be used with the writing process.

The following presents information about each kind of writing approach that you may use with your children.

- **Language Experience Approach** The teacher acts as a scribe and records children's ideas in a group setting. This approach allows children to openly express themselves through oral language and not feel threatened because they do not yet possess the mechanics of written language.

- **Shared Writing** The teacher works with a small group of children, placing the emphasis on the composing process. The teacher and children work together to plan the text, and then the teacher acts as facilitator to help children develop and organize ideas.

- **Interactive Writing** Shared writing and interactive writing are similar processes except that in interactive writing the teacher and the children "share the pen." The teacher determines when to involve children in the writing based on the focus of instruction. The teacher models the writing form and shapes children's language through prompts that help them write words and phrases.

- **Guided Writing** The teacher offers assistance by guiding children's writing, responding to it, and extending children's thinking in the composing process. Guided writing may happen during whole-class, small-group, or one-on-one sessions. The teacher's role is one of facilitator, helping children discover what they want to say and how to clearly write it.

Interactive Writing

Interactive writing is a form of assisted writing or scaffolded instruction. Interactive writing is a process in which the teacher and children compose and construct a written message. The teacher acts as a model, demonstrating the writing process of composing texts, while both the teacher and children scribe.

Interactive writing includes these stages.

- **Construct the Text** After the teacher and children determine their purpose and audience, they "share the pen," writing the text together letter by letter or word by word. This allows the children to think about how they are using language to communicate meaning. Then the teacher or the children direct attention to particular features of words and talk about them.

- **Reread, Revise, and Proofread** These steps serve as an opportunity to clarify and enhance the meaning of texts. They also teach children to:
  - check their work as they write
  - recognize the importance of conventions
  - check the meaning of the text

- **Revisit the Text** It is important to revisit the text to focus on concepts related to word solving. Word solving helps children figure out unfamiliar words as they read and spell words as they write. The teacher should help children
  - notice that some words look like other words
  - recognize word parts
  - connect words by how they look

Writer's Companion
Approaches to Writing Instruction

The Writing Center

AUTHOR'S CHAIR Place a chair in a prominent place. As each child's writing is shared, have him or her sit there. Make available a rug or cushions for the audience to sit on.

SHARING BASKET Provide a basket in which children can place a piece of writing they are willing to share.

PORTFOLIOS Store children's portfolios in boxes or crates. Organize them alphabetically by first name. Each individual portfolio should be expandable. Some examples are:
- accordion folders
- pocket folders
- manila folders with yarn extenders attached to each side

PICTURE BOX Folders organized by topic can hold pictures cut from magazines, brochures, ad circulars, and coloring books. Children can help themselves to the pictures as they write or publish their work.

WORD WALL Strategically place your Word Wall so children have access to it while writing.

WORK TABLE A large work space with labeled bins is ideal. Bins may hold writing and book-making materials. Consider the following:
- white and colored paper
- stationery, cards, self-stick labels
- blank books
- lead and colored pencils
- pens, markers, crayons
- glue sticks, tape, staplers, rulers
- yarn, brass fasteners
- a hole punch, pencil sharpeners
- a date stamp, rubber stamps, and ink pads

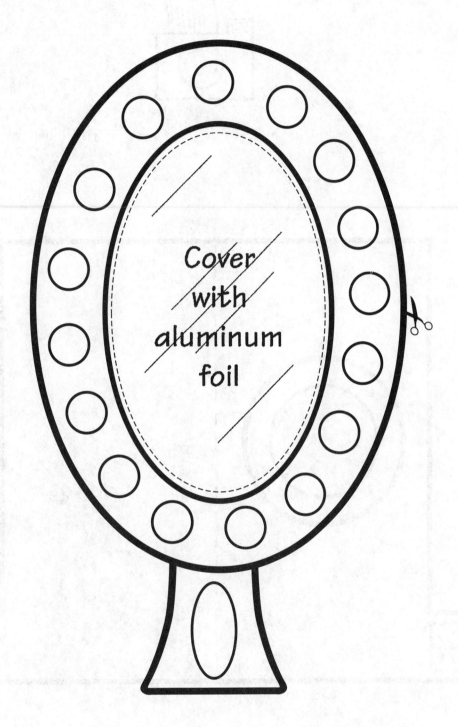

Cover
with
aluminum
foil

Have children cut out mirrors and decorate. Give them each a piece of aluminum foil to glue into the center so they can see their reflections. Children can use the mirrors to help them tell about themselves.

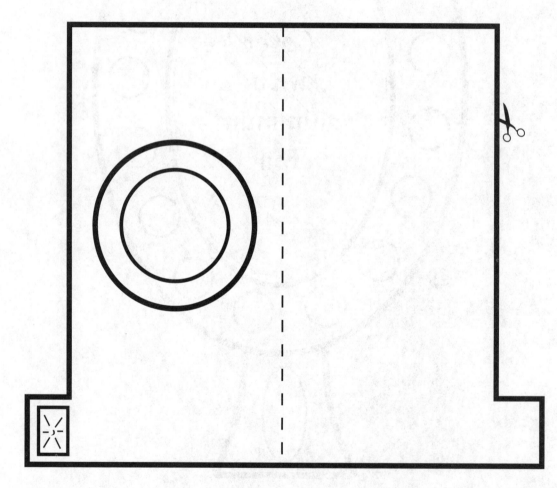

Have children "take pictures" that will help them brainstorm for a writing project. Children should cut out, fold, and staple the edges, leaving one edge open so that the pictures they draw on index cards can be stored inside the camera pocket.

Writer's Companion

Patterns for Story Starters and Presentation

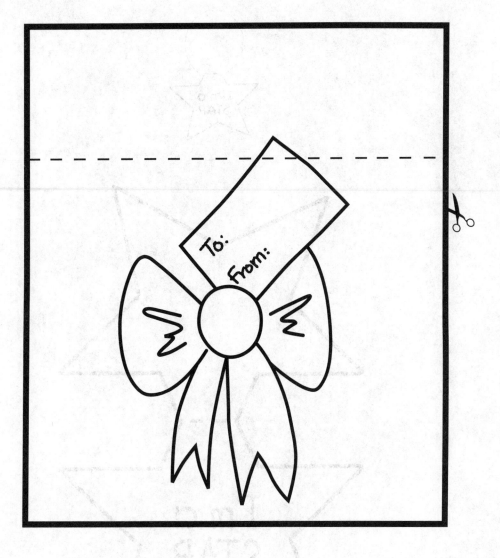

Have children cut out the pattern and then glue it above the dotted line onto another piece of paper the same size. Ask children to draw a picture under the flap of the perfect surprise gift. Have them share their pictures with the class.

Have children cut out the star and decorate it with glitter. Fold the star and glue the bottom, leaving room at the top to string yarn through to make a necklace. Have children talk about why they are "stars."

Handwriting

Individual children enter school with various levels of handwriting skills, but they all have the desire to communicate effectively. To learn correct letter formation, they must be familiar with the concepts of:

- position (top, middle, bottom; on, above, below)
- size (tall, short)
- direction (left, right; up, down; over, around, across)
- order (first, next, then, last)
- open and closed
- spacing`

To assess children's handwriting skills, have them write each capital and lowercase letter of the alphabet. Note whether children use correct formation, appropriate size, and spacing.

Stroke and Letter Formation

The shape and formation of letters shown on the following pages is based on the way experienced writers write their letters. Most letters are formed with a continuous stroke. Letter formation should be simplified through the use of "letter talk"—an oral description of how the letter is formed. Models for manuscript and D'Nealian Handwriting are provided to support different writing systems.

Learning Modes

A visual, kinesthetic, tactile, and auditory approach should be used. To help children internalize letter forms, each letter should be taught in the context of how it looks, the sound it stands for, and how it is formed.

Handwriting

Position for Writing

Establishing the correct posture, pencil grip, and paper position for writing will help prevent handwriting problems later on.

Posture Children should sit with both feet on the floor and with hips to the back of the chair. They can lean forward slightly but should not slouch. The writing surface should be smooth and flat and at a height that allows the upper arms to be perpendicular to the surface and the elbows to be under the shoulders.

Writing Instrument An adult-sized number-two lead pencil is a satisfactory writing tool for most children. However, use your judgment in determining what type of instrument is most suitable for each child, given his or her level of development.

Hand Dominance To determine each child's hand dominance, observe him or her at play and note which hand is the preferred hand. Watching the child turn a doorknob, roll a ball, build a block tower, or turn the pages in a book will help you note hand dominance.

Paper Position and Pencil Grip The paper should be slanted along the line of each child's writing arm. Children use their non-writing hand to hold their paper in place. Children should hold their pencils slightly above the paint lines—about one inch from the lead tips.

Handwriting

 Reaching All Learners

The best instruction builds on what children already know and can do. Given the tremendous range in children's experience with writing materials prior to entering school, a variety of approaches will be needed.

Extra Support For children with limited print concepts, one of the first and most important understandings is that print carries meaning and that writing has real purpose. Provide many opportunities for writing in natural settings. For example, children can:

- make a class directory, listing names and phone numbers of their classmates

- record observations in science

- write and illustrate labels for art materials

- draw and label maps, pictures, graphs, and picture dictionaries

English Language Learners These learners can also participate in meaningful print experiences. They can:

- write signs, name tags, and messages

- label pictures

- join in shared writing experiences

Advanced To ensure the continued rapid advancement of children who enter school already writing:

- Expose children to a wide range of reading materials.

- Provide opportunities for independent writing on self-selected and assigned topics.

- Provide explicit instruction in print conventions (punctuation, use of capital letters).

- Introduce simple editing marks, and encourage children to proofread and edit their own work.

© Harcourt

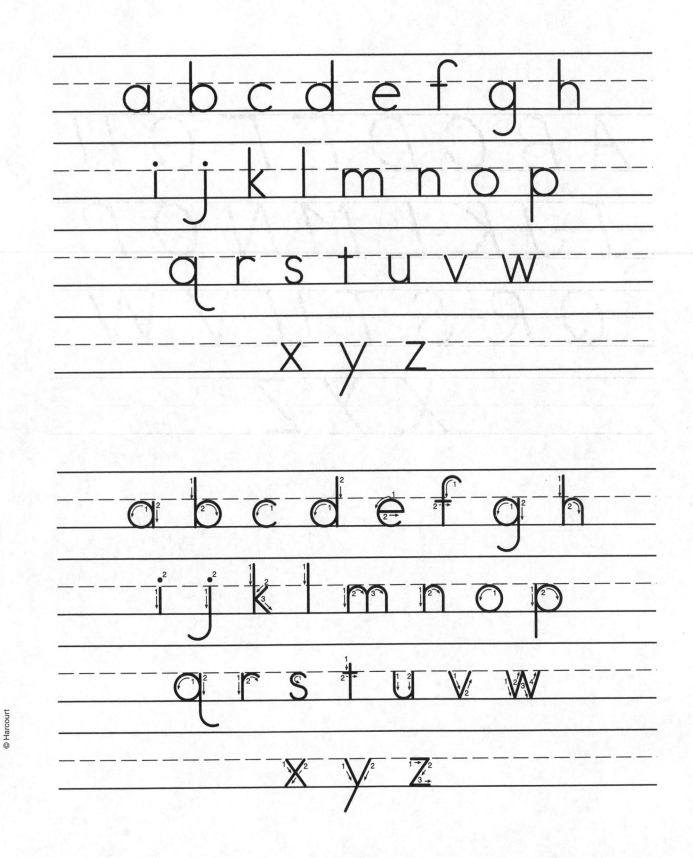

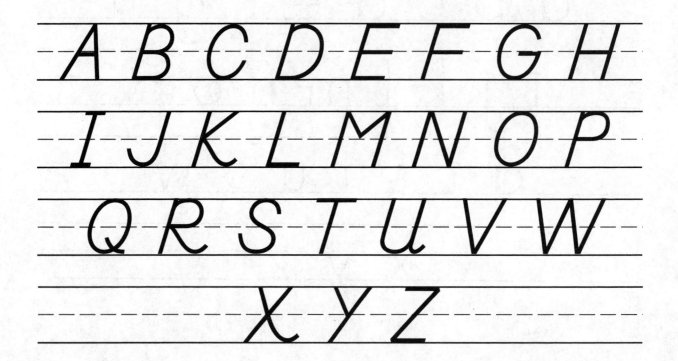

a b c d e f g h

i j k l m n o p

q r s t u v w

x y z

Writer's Companion
Handwriting Models

Print Awareness, Handwriting, and Technology Checklist

Child _____ Teacher _____ Grade _____

	Date ___	Date ___	Date ___	Date ___	Date ___	Date ___
PRINT AWARENESS						
Understands that spoken words are represented in written language by specific sequences of letters						
Names, matches, and produces all letters of the alphabet, uppercase and lowercase						
Knows the order of the alphabet						
Tracks print						
Knows print concepts: letters, words, sentences, questions, capitalization, and end marks						
HANDWRITING						
Writes his/her own name and other important words						
Writes each letter of the alphabet, both capital and lowercase, using correct formation, appropriate size, and spacing						
Writes messages that move left-to-right and top-to-bottom on the page						
Shows an increasing control of pencil grip						
Shows an increasing control of paper position						
Shows an increasing control of stroke						
Shows an increasing control of posture						
Uses word and letter spacing to make messages readable						
Leaves margins						
TECHNOLOGY						
Shows awareness of the uses of available technology, such as word processing, spell-checking, and printing						
Uses available technology to support aspects of writing						

Comments:

KEY:

N = Not Observed

O = Observed Occasionally

R = Observed Regularly

© Harcourt

Writer's Companion
Assessment Checklists

Writing Conference Checklist

Child _____ Teacher _____ Grade _____

	Date ___	Date ___	Date ___	Date ___	Date ___	Date ___
CONTENT AND ORGANIZATION						
Expresses ideas, details, and topics						
Writes stories through dictation, pictures, and writing						
Aims for a purpose and an audience for pictures and writing						
Constructs several sentences on one topic in a logical order						
Uses a variety of prewriting strategies						
Publishes compositions in a variety of ways						
Uses personal experiences as a source of writing ideas						
CONVENTIONS AND MECHANICS						
Writes legible manuscript letters						
Writes with left-to-right, top-to-bottom directionality						
Uses appropriate spacing between words, sentences						
Writes in mostly complete sentences						
Uses beginning capitalization						
Uses appropriate end punctuation in sentences						
SPELLING						
Produces phonetically related approximations						
Spells some high-frequency words correctly in connected writing						

Comments:

KEY:

N = Not Observed

O = Observed Occasionally

R = Observed Regularly

Grammar-in-Writing Checklist

Child _____ Teacher _____ Grade _____

	Date _____	Date _____	Date _____	Date _____	Date _____	Date _____
GRAMMAR AND USAGE						
Uses nouns and verbs in sentences						
Composes complete sentences						
Edits toward standard grammar and usage in final drafts						
Composes sentences with describing words						
Composes sentences with details						
Uses pronouns correctly						
Uses correct forms and tenses of *to be*						
MECHANICS						
Spells using phonetically related approximations that can generally be read by others						
Uses basic punctuation correctly						
Uses capitalization at the beginning of sentences and some proper nouns						
ORAL LANGUAGE						
Shows increasing control of grammar when speaking						

Comments:

KEY:

N = Not Observed

O = Observed Occasionally

R = Observed Regularly